"Ron Boehme has brought an ⟨...⟩ f what is next for global missions. Missionaries in the twenty-first century, far from being strait-laced Victorian folk in pith-helmets, are likely to be young Koreans, adventurous Africans, guitar-playing Brazilians, and even computer-savvy Chinese.... *The Fourth Wave* is required reading for anyone who wants to know why Christianity was able to expand globally in the past, and how it is likely to continue its exciting journey in the years ahead."

David Aikman, former *Time* magazine correspondent and author of *Jesus in Beijing*

"What has God done to win the world over in the past twenty centuries? What is God going to do in the twenty-first century? Ron Boehme answers both questions in *The Fourth Wave*. I encourage you to ride the wave God is surging in our generation! ... This is a book about faith in God and high hope for tomorrow."

Leith Anderson, president, National Association of Evangelicals (USA)

"The global landscape has been dramatically altered over the last several years, and Ron Boehme has provided a new road map for the church.... Anyone pursuing a fresh perspective that makes room for current realities will find this book incredibly helpful. Embrace this new wineskin and be prepared for a bold awakening to God's plan for this hour!"

Glenn C. Burris Jr., president, The Foursquare Church

"*The Fourth Wave* is a visionary look at the acts of the Holy Spirit in this era of missions history. From everywhere to everywhere—including every ethnicity, religious background, and sphere of society—the face of missions is changing rapidly. This book is faith-stretching and forward-looking. You will be blessed by it!"

Paul Eshleman, vice president, Campus Crusade for Christ International

"Jesus once rebuked the scribes and Pharisees because they didn't understand the signs of the times. Ron has done a lot of research and given a great deal of thought to the tidal changes that are happening right now in our understanding of and approach to the Great Commission. Every serious Christian should read this book and use it as a point of discussion. We need to wrestle together with these issues so that the body of Christ can cooperate fully with God in what He's doing in our generation."

Jim Stier, field director of the Americas, Youth With A Mission

"My colleague Ron Boehme has lived and learned missions for decades. Not only is he qualified to bring us a glimpse of the future of Christian outreach, but this work calls us to be a part of it. This book is fascinating, educating, and motivating.... God has laid a foundation through wonderful missionary leaders and organizations so that every Christian could finish the task!"

Joel C. Hunter, senior pastor, Northland, A Church Distributed

"If I had only one word to describe Ron Boehme's *The Fourth Wave*, it would be perspective. . . . Each wave of God's redemptive thrusts throughout history is uniquely described, but they are all drawn together by five common factors which give a unifying perspective. *The Fourth Wave* is comprehensive and insightful. At the same time, it is practical and personal, filled with stories, examples, and applications. . . . I heartily recommend this unique missions resource."

Paul Fleischmann, president, National Network of Youth Ministries (USA)

"There is a mighty wave covering the earth today, more like a tsunami than a wave. It has swept hundreds of millions of people into God's kingdom and is leading to the transformation of whole spheres of society and entire nations. We are living in the time of the greatest revival in the history of the church. *The Fourth Wave* tells the story of this mighty movement of movements—it is an inspiring, captivating read!"

Floyd McClung, founder, All Nations, Capetown, South Africa

"In a recent *Foreign Affairs* magazine on the world ahead I read in the article 'The Globalized God' that 'the most dramatic religious explosion in the world today is the spread of Pentecostalism and evangelical Protestantism.' But there is much more ahead! *The Fourth Wave* describes another wave—a coming global mission explosion that is spiritual, relational, integrative, and innovative in nature and will further expand the Kingdom of God."

Dr. Jesse Miranda, CEO, National Hispanic Christian Leadership Conference; president, Miranda Center for Hispanic Leadership

"Building on a captivating overview of the history of mission, Ron Boehme paints a compelling picture of the next surge of Great Commission activity. The ocean swell of this Fourth Wave is already in view, and the powerful stories in this book inspire faith toward the day when 'the earth will be filled with the knowledge of the glory of the LORD, as the waters cover the sea.'"

Steve Moore, president and CEO, The Mission Exchange; author of *Who Is My Neighbor?*

"My favorite graduate course to teach is 'The Role of Students in Revivals and Awakenings.' I have enjoyed teaching a unit in that course on the successive waves of missions. But reading Ron Boehme's *The Fourth Wave* sent me to school. My teaching content now will be far richer. And personally, Ron Boehme has prompted me to watch for new ways to join Christ in making His name more famous in all the earth. . . . I deeply desire to see a young generation worldwide mobilized to take the Good News to the final groups on the planet. *The Fourth Wave* has poured gasoline on that dream."

Richard Ross, professor of student ministry, Southwestern Seminary; cofounder, True Love Waits

"It is not uncommon today for 'missions' to be defined in terms of a summer outreach or a second-year course at Bible school. . . . Ron Boehme's latest book, *The Fourth Wave*, changes this perception. Readers are immediately struck by a sense of epic drama—and universal call. . . . It would be easy to get lost in the sweeping themes *The Fourth Wave* deals with, but Ron is a clever and sure-footed guide. "

George Otis Jr., producer, Transformations Documentaries

"We can't know all of what God is doing or wants to do. *The Fourth Wave* give us a glimpse of what He's done in the past and is doing today. . . . You will discover ministries and people you've never heard of who are doing amazing things. But most importantly, you may discover how you can have a greater part in God's expanding Kingdom work."

Greg H. Parsons, global director, U.S. Center for World Mission

"As a student of history I have always suspected that God was controlling human events through divine providence to fulfill His eternal mission of reaching the nations. Ron Boehme has written a fascinating overview of missions history to capture the reality of God's sovereignty over the nations. *The Fourth Wave* reflects global evangelism from the New Testament to current movements that are bringing us closer to completion of the Great Commission."

Jerry Rankin, president emeritus, International Mission Board, Southern Baptist Convention

"What a timely book for this generation and final era of missions! . . . Cutting-edge insights based on amazing accounts of God's marvelous work [are] combined with historical insights that put it all in God's kingdom perspective. I am absolutely thrilled by Ron's book, and knowing Ron personally, I am doubly excited about him writing this from a passionate heart for Jesus and His kingdom purposes."

Nancy M. Wilson, global ambassador, Campus Crusade for Christ International

"If you're interested in seeing what the fourth wave of missions looks like, read this book. It will excite you about all God has done in the past and will challenge you to reconsider your future. This book is a grand slam!"

Peter Iliyn, North American leader, Youth With A Mission

"My friend Ron Boehme has always been an accurate seer and an articulate presenter. . . . In *The Fourth Wave* he absolutely nails the timeline of God's Spirit bringing God's love, power, and good news to all humanity. I've seen the future and am excited. . . . Good-bye to antiquated, even hindering, methods, models, and vocabulary. Welcome to the life-giving river that flows everywhere it is needed, and under no other control but God's. Read about it, then jump in."

Dean Sherman, author of *Relationships* and *Spiritual Warfare for Every Christian*

"I have spent most of my life training the young generation who are the future of world evangelism. Increasingly, that training takes me to many nations where God is at work. Ron's book really helped me understand the historical footprints of God's missionary enterprise and why the next step will be an exponential explosion of Fourth Wave missionaries. . . . This is history as it was meant to be told—with a big hook to help you find your place in the current chapter."

Barry St. Clair, president, Reach Out Youth Solutions

"This is a timely, must-read book, which Ron Boehme has written for anyone who desires a modern-day book of Acts experience. His well-documented analysis of church history is clear, and his prophetic insightfulness lays out a Spirit-led roadmap for all who long to be genuinely fruitful Christians with an understanding of the great opportunities which God is giving to His church at this moment in time."

Jim Tolle, pastor and church planter, The Church On The Way, Los Angeles

"Ron Boehme's new book, *The Fourth Wave*, is outstanding and well worth reading, studying, and reflecting upon. He includes a lot of good research, but he also writes from an amazing personal knowledge and experience of the mission world. My prayer is that *The Fourth Wave* will receive wide distribution and become a momentum builder in the mission movement and completion of the Great Commission."

Jerry N. Wiles, president emeritus, Living Water International

"I met Ron Boehme when I first came to Washington, DC, in 1981. . . . In the years since, as my own travels have taken me to 130 nations around the world, I have grown to appreciate Ron's friendship and heart for Jesus the Messiah. Ron is right that a fresh movement has begun that will greatly enlarge the family of God. I see it everywhere I go. My own particular burden is for Africa and the Middle East. I encourage you to read Ron's book and find yours. This book is loaded with inspiration and practical tools to help you get there."

Mark Siljander, former member of the U.S. Congress; U.S. Ambassador to the United Nations (Alt. Delegate)

"Ron Boehme's new book, *The Fourth Wave*, stirred me deeply about what God has done in past missions history in preparation for a vast worldwide outpouring of the Holy Spirit today. Many things are converging—and God is at the center of it to introduce the peoples of the world to his Son, the Lord Jesus. Read this book and find your own niche in the current Kingdom harvest. God has a place for you, your family, and your church. Don't miss it."

George Wood, general superintendent, Assemblies of God (USA)

THE
FOURTH
WAVE

TAKING YOUR PLACE
IN THE NEW ERA OF MISSIONS

RON BOEHME

YWAM PUBLISHING
Seattle, Washington

YWAM Publishing is the publishing ministry of Youth With A Mission. Youth With A Mission (YWAM) is an international missionary organization of Christians from many denominations dedicated to presenting Jesus Christ to this generation. To this end, YWAM has focused its efforts in three main areas: (1) training and equipping believers for their part in fulfilling the Great Commission (Matthew 28:19), (2) personal evangelism, and (3) mercy ministry (medical and relief work).

For a free catalog of books and materials, call (425) 771-1153 or (800) 922-2143. Visit us online at www.ywampublishing.com.

The Fourth Wave: Taking Your Place in the New Era of Missions
Copyright © 2011 by Ron Boehme

Published by YWAM Publishing
a ministry of Youth With A Mission
P.O. Box 55787, Seattle, WA 98155

First printing 2011

Library of Congress Cataloging-in-Publication Data is on file with the publisher and the Library of Congress.

ISBN 978-1-57658-555-9

Printed in the United States of America

To Enkhsuren, my Mongolian daughter,
Bold and Dorjhand,
Sodoo and Aldaraa,
and to the first generation church in Mongolia.

You are the new face of missions,
bringing great delight to your Heavenly Father.
May you walk triumphantly on the shoulders of those who have gone before.

TO ORDER MORE BOOKS
GO TO:
www.usrenewal.org

Contents

Acknowledgments

I am not the most qualified person to write this book; however, the decision to complete a master's degree gave me a jump start on the necessary research during the winter and spring of 2010. With the help of many, a thesis on *The Fourth Wave* was completed at Northwest University in Kirkland, Washington, in May 2010.

Thirty-seven years of missions service preceded the thesis and book. I am deeply thankful for Youth With A Mission, its courageous and committed leaders and thousands of workers worldwide who have contributed to my vision over the past four decades. Special thanks are due to Loren Cunningham, Leland Paris, Lynn Green, and Peter Iliyn for their leadership influence and trust. I would have nothing to say on this subject if I had not bumped into YWAM in New Zealand in fall of 1972. That story is contained in chapter 1.

I would like to thank the members of our inaugural NU Missional Leadership cohort—Ray and Sandy Jennings, Nick Buehler, Bethany von Steinbergs, Tyson DeVries, Dale Oquist, Dave Westman, Andrew Fox, Jeff Duchemin, and Fred Boyd—for their passion for Christian leadership, the enjoyment of our friendships, and fiery discussions during our master's course, all of which led to this project. I'm grateful to Joe and Nancy Saggio for providing both hospitality and strong direction in our studies. I'd also like to thank Ed and Sue Giaimo for many stimulating discussions and the use of their home during various weeks of study in Kirkland.

I'd like to thank all the good folks at YWAM Publishing for their vision and excellent work on this project, especially Tom Bragg, Warren Walsh, Ryan Davis, and Luann Anderson, along with Mary Calvez and

Nancy Aguilar, for their fine editorial help and final reshaping of the man-uscript. Special thanks are due to my parents, Robert and Mary Boehme, for their unending support in this project, including Dad's editing skills. Also to Lori Varick for her excellent editorial contribution. And to my wonderful wife, Shirley, who is my partner in life and mission. To God be the glory for his marvelous waves of salvation that reach their crescendo in Jesus Christ, who is now sending his redeemed friends to the ends of the earth.

Foreword

Coincidentally, on the morning I received the manuscript for Ron Boehme's new book, I was teaching a class on missions history and was expressing my frustration to the students on my inability to properly treat such a worthy subject in my allotted time. I came home to peruse *The Fourth Wave* and found it a refreshing river of succinct, detailed, passionate, and prophetic insight into the subject of global missions.

Ron's keen analysis is fed by streams originating in inspiring stories, biblical truth, and a strong forward challenge to reach the world for Jesus. Ron's nearly forty years of hands-on involvement in the missionary task and his well-known Bible teaching skills make *The Fourth Wave* a must read for salty ole surfers like myself. Maybe you, too. We all need, as General William Booth put it, "a kick in the pants" to become future generations of seafaring young wave riders who dare to wax-up, paddle out, turn around, and catch the Fourth Wave.

Jesus indicated that we find the treasures of godly wisdom by blending what we have learned in the past (the old) with what we hear God speaking to us in the present (the new). "Every teacher of religious law who becomes a disciple in the Kingdom of Heaven is like a homeowner who brings from his storeroom new gems of truth as well as old" (Matt. 13:52). This book nails both: Ron encourages us by telling the stories of what God has done in missions history and then challenges us to step into an exciting new future.

Revival movements fail when either the old fails to see what God is doing in the present or the new, blinded by the present awakening, fails to realize that they are standing on the shoulders of the giants of revival history. Ron demonstrates that those who ride God's current wave of missional outreach will have this wisdom to guide their maneuvers around the sharks and other deep-sea predators that smell the blood-bought riders of God's final wave to the nations.

The closest we in the West have come to revival in our recent past is the Jesus movement and its cousin, the charismatic movement. While neither is viewed by historians as a full-blown awakening, they both contained elements of the great revivals in our history. With forty years of history we can now see again the wisdom of Jesus' words. The streams of renewal that were grounded on "the faith that was once for all entrusted to the saints" (Jude 3 NIV) prospered and grew. Those impressed with the present at the expense of the past were soon the victims of their own pride.

Jesus gave wide berth for new wineskins to contain the new wine of fresh moves of his Holy Spirit. Throughout history God has demonstrated that he honors those who create new containers for his wine. He seems to delight in the bold, brash, fresh initiatives of the young ("your sons and daughters will prophesy . . . your young men will see visions . . .") as long as they appreciate their history and the "dreams of the old" (Acts 2:17–21). The Fourth Wave gives us a manifesto for the revival we know we all need—a multi-generational move of God that will amaze even the angels.

I live a thirty minute's drive from where some of the largest, most powerful waves in the world can be found—Oahu's North Shore. These moving mountains are generated by storms thousands of miles away that traverse the Pacific when coupled with the right wind conditions. These giant waves give delight to those few brave souls called big-wave surfers who dare ride them. It is said that a wave at Waimea Bay contains enough energy to light New York City for a week. May the God who is "mightier than the waves of the sea" (Ps. 93:4 ESV) create a missions wave that we can all ride, containing the living water of his Spirit that will refresh the nations.

Weekend warriors and beach sitters are a dime a dozen. Don't be one. Read Ron Boehme's The Fourth Wave and take your place in God's building tsunami of Christ's love for the nations.

Danny Lehmann
Youth With A Mission, Hawaiian Islands

Introduction

It's all about salvation—on a global scale.

God has always had a plan to reach every person in the world with his love and forgiveness through the death and resurrection of Jesus Christ. We call his outreach *missions*.

As a thirty-seven-year career missionary in Youth With A Mission (YWAM), I have believed for many decades that the focus of history *is* missions. In pursuit of that goal, I've had the privilege of sharing Christ in over sixty nations of the world since 1970. During that time, the face of missions has changed greatly. We will explore those changes and their implications in the coming pages.

Different words or phrases have been used over the past two thousand years to describe the advance of world evangelism. The apostle Paul and the early Christians talked about their "mission" to share Christ in Jerusalem, Judea, and to the ends of the earth (Acts 1:8 and 21:19).[1] After the advance of the church through the Middle Ages, it became popular to describe sharing your faith cross-culturally as engaging in "missions."[2] Today, being "missional" is the phrase of choice for many of those engaging others with the claims of Christ.[3] For the purposes of this book, I will use all three of these terms synonymously to describe the advance of Christian faith in the nations—while highlighting the newer term of being "missional."

In this book, I will examine current trends in world evangelization that have been built upon two thousand years of missionary enterprise. What kind of twenty-first century mission force is God raising up to complete the Great Commission? What will be the makeup and focus of a trend many are calling the *fourth wave of modern missions*?

My research leads me to conclude that the coming wave of missions will build upon all the strengths of the past, yet usher in a new era of individual participation unseen in past moves of God. The book will discuss at length

- how past waves of evangelization have set the stage for the current move of the Holy Spirit around the world;
- how the past three waves of modern missions were necessary to bring about the fourth;
- what types of people and nations will be involved;
- what the fruit of this latest wave of God's love among the nations might be.

I have used three different research methods to analyze trends in modern mission and where the future is leading us. *Historical:* There is much that we can learn from the past moves of God in the history of missions. There is a great treasure trove of literature on this subject for which I am grateful. I will lean on the writings of historians and missiologists who have chronicled the past as predictors of the future. *Conceptual:* Predicting the future is somewhat predicated on past historical trends, but ultimately lies in the realm of conjecture. In my thirty-seven years as a missionary, an evolving concept of the missional future has been growing in my heart and mind as I've watched a new form of missionary emerge in many parts of the world. *Theological:* Missions is a part of the "study of God" that theology encompasses. Missiology is a vital element of theology in understanding God's work on the earth, for God is in the people business (John 3:16).

The data necessary for this project has been drawn from books, articles, websites, conferences, teachings, and mission statistics compiled by historians and missions leaders in many parts of the world. I have drawn heavily on certain experts in these fields, including Kenneth Scott Latourette, Ruth A. Tucker, David Barrett, Todd Johnson, Patrick Johnstone, Ralph Winter, and the publications of some of the world's largest global missionary societies.

I have also leaned heavily on the perspective of various authors and missiologists in the field on current and future missions. I hope that my extensive international research in the field balances my Western missions literary bias.

I believe that both the biblical narrative and the history of the expansion of the gospel since that time can be best explained through various "waves" of evangelism that the Holy Spirit has orchestrated—even beginning in Old Testament times (chapter 2). The Day of Pentecost launched the first wave of Christian advance as early Jewish Christians shared the good news of Christ with fellow Jews in Jerusalem, and thousands came into the church. The kingdom of God then spread to the Gentiles through Peter's visit to the house of Cornelius and the growth of faith among non-Jews through the Apostle Paul. After centuries of persecution, the waves of Christian evangelism had permeated the entire Roman Empire (chapter 3).

During the Middle Ages, various monks and monasteries led the advance of the Christian faith. Later on, missional activity surged forward in Europe, including the biblical rediscoveries of the Protestant Reformation and a corresponding Counter-Reformation in the Catholic Church. However, according to missiologist Ralph Winter, founder of the U.S. Center for World Mission, modern day missions began in 1792 when William Carey, the first Protestant missionary, sailed to India.[4] This first wave of modern missions focused on the *coastlands* of the world (chapter 5).

The second wave of modern missions began in the nineteenth century with David Livingstone's groundbreaking exploration of the African interior and other missionaries, such as Hudson Taylor, also sharing the gospel in the inner regions of China. Missional advance was going global at this time, having started in the seaports of the world and then moving *inland* (chapter 6).[5]

During the twentieth century, missions focus progressed from the coastlands and interiors to a third wave of missions outreach among unreached people groups, numbering thirteen thousand globally (chapter 7).[6] At the time of this writing, there are fewer than one thousand people groups in the world that are untargeted and unengaged with missionary activity. Over two billion people worldwide profess faith in Christ. Yet, there are approximately another two billion people in the world, primarily Muslims, Buddhists, and Hindus, who have not been evangelized.[7]

Past moves of God and three waves of modern missions have set the stage for a final harvest (chapters 8 and 9). I believe a *fourth wave of modern missions has begun*—and that wave will involve the following: people of all ages and all nationalities reaching everyone in the world with the good news, using innovative technologies and relational approaches in all spheres of life. This new wave will be the subject of chapters 10 through 16.

The fourth wave of modern missions has profound implications for the church—each one of us. Here's the bottom line: for the first time in history, believers from every nation on earth can be missional. As the Protestant Reformation restored the concept of the priesthood of all believers, the Fourth Wave will restore the idea that every believer is called to be missional—to go and make disciples of all nations.

I believe with all my heart that you, like millions of others who believe in Jesus and are looking for God's direction in their lives, will find your divine destiny on the crest of this wave. This book was written to help you prepare to get up and ride the surf.

You were born for such a time as this (Esther 4:14).

Part 1

History Is "His Story"

"World missions was on God's mind from the beginning."

—Dave Davidson

"Christian missionary work is the most difficult thing in the world. It is surprising that it should ever have been attempted."

—Stephen Neill

"God is pursuing with omnipotent passion a world-wide purpose of gathering joyful worshipers for Himself from every tribe and tongue and people and nation. He has an inexhaustible enthusiasm for the supremacy of His name among the nations. Therefore, let us bring our affections into line with His, and, for the sake of His name, let us renounce the quest for worldly comforts and join His global purpose."

—John Piper

Chapter 1

Sea Change

WE LIVE IN AN ERA of amazing change:

- Urbanization—people moving to cities
- Globalization—our economies and cultures becoming linked together
- Exploding population growth—heading for double digit billions
- Technological wizardry—got the latest "app" yet?
- Clashes of cultures, numerous wars
- The greatest hopes, dreams, concerns, and fears of all time

I believe the greatest changes are still coming. A sea change of activity will take center stage in the twenty-first century. One of these changes will be more important than the others: *the Fourth Wave.*

A profound transformation.

"Sea change" is a helpful metaphor because sometimes it is subtle, unnoticed. I remember watching the fall of the Iron Curtain on television in 1989 from a conference setting near Niagara Falls, New York. This profound change in the history of Soviet communism, especially affecting the nations of Europe, had been a slow, rising tide that very few noticed or predicted. Interestingly, I had seen this change coming three years before the event.[1]

Some sea changes build slowly or silently. The cycles of El Niño and La Niña (the fluctuation in Pacific Ocean temperatures that have a great impact on global climate) take years to reach their peaks and then move in the opposite direction. The 2004 Indian Ocean tsunami which struck Indonesia, Sri Lanka, and other Asian nations, was the result of the second largest recorded earthquake in history (9.1 to 9.3 on the Richter scale), whose duration was the longest in recorded history (8.3 to 10 minutes). It silently sent monstrous waves of up to one hundred feet crashing down on a number of Asian nations, killing approximately 230,000 people. They didn't see it coming.

I believe most people in the church and the world at large don't see the great sea change that has taken place in Christian missions over the past few decades. A new wave of world evangelization is beginning to race across the "national oceans" of the world, something missiologists are describing as the fourth wave of modern missions. Youth With A Mission (YWAM) is a vivid example of that sea change.

When I joined YWAM in the early 1970s, we were a primarily white, middle-class missionary society made up of three hundred full-time workers. Today YWAM has over sixteen thousand full-time staff from over 150 countries working in nearly every nation on earth—whose members are 60 percent people of color.[2]

Is this change indicative of a major shift in the focus of twenty-first century missions? I believe that it is—and you can be a part of it.

In this chapter I'd like you to visit some "real life exhibits" that punctuate the profound changes that are occurring in missions. As you ponder each story, see if you can guess which nation or region of the world is being described before you get to the punch line.

Let's begin our tour with Exhibit A.

From Rags to Riches

During the 1950s, this nation was one of the poorest in its region of the world. It had a long history of spiritual darkness and foreign conquest and was now reduced to rubble by a war that carried its name.[3]

One hundred years before the war, Christian missionaries had arrived in the land—hundreds of them from over a dozen nations. They pioneered some of the first schools, newspapers, hospitals, and churches this nation had ever known. Many of these missionaries died young due to disease and harsh resistance. But a foundation had been laid.

In 1907 the nation had experienced a powerful spiritual revival in the north—emanating from its largest city which was called at the time the "Jerusalem of the East."[4] However, fifty years later the war came—and the landscape was reduced to ashes. The future looked very bleak.

Then, in one generation, God's mission seeds began to grow. Through amazing revival, prayer, hard work, and modernization, this beaten, broken nation became one of the most born-again, missionary-minded, and wealthiest nations in all of Asia. The explosion of the Christian faith in this nation has certainly contributed to its amazing transformation over the past few decades.

Today South Korea is an Asian Tiger because its people encountered the "Lion of Judah"—Jesus and his missional friends—during the third wave of modern missions (which we discuss in chapter 7).

I learned the incredible story of South Korea, its churches, and its global mission outreach through various trips to that nation. We prayed in the sanctuary of Yoido Full Gospel Church—the world's largest congregation, with over eight hundred thousand members.[5] We toured the Yanghwajin Missionary Cemetery, a small plot of land among Seoul's many skyscrapers, where 517 missionaries from thirteen different nations are honored for their sacrificial service.[6]

Korea currently boasts a number of the largest churches in the world and is the world's sixth largest Christian missionary-sending nation (ahead of Great Britain, Germany, and Canada). Korean believers have a vision for sending out one hundred thousand missionaries by 2030. *Koreans will be a part of the Fourth Wave.*

But we must move on to Exhibit B.

From Backward to Forward-Looking

It's hard to believe that even after the Age of Exploration this nation was relatively unknown until the early 1800s, and even then was open to outsiders on a limited basis. Though an ambitious fifteenth-century leader launched large trading ships all over the world (some containing up to four thousand passengers), and discovered America seventy years before Christopher Columbus,[7] his exploits were lost to history, and the nation remained in constant upheaval and spiritual darkness.

A violent twentieth-century revolution in the land sent millions to their deaths and further isolated this nation from the developing world. However, in the 1970s God began to water the seeds of a century and a half of missionary outreach throughout the countryside and brought revival under great persecution, poverty, and suffering. That revival swept the rural areas of the nation and later ignited in the cities. A parallel thrust of industrial modernization catapulted this nation to the forefront of the twenty-first century.

Today this recently backward nation—China—has become a spiritual and economic powerhouse, with more Christian evangelicals than the United States[8] and the world's second largest economy.[9] Chinese Christians share a vision to send millions of missionaries across Central Asia (the *Back to Jerusalem* movement, which will be discussed in chapter 8).

I've taken trips to China for a number of years and am excited about its future. In 2008 I visited the Temple of Heaven in the center of Beijing during the Olympic Games and thought about the Ming emperor Zhu Di (dynastic title Yongle) who had called the world to this site in 1421. To extend his invitation, he sent 250 treasure ships and 3,500 other vessels across the oceans. Most of them never returned. A few months after their departure, Beijing was struck by lightning and burned to the ground. China then slid into chaos and darkness for hundreds of years—only emerging in the late twentieth century.

As we stood in the ornate garden of the Temple of Heaven, a young Chinese woman came to meditate and pray at its entrance. We learned that she was seeking the Living God—and we prayed with her and shared encouragement. She is representative of over one billion Chinese whose destiny and twenty-first century role is being defined. This seems certain: *Chinese believers will be a part of the Fourth Wave.*

Similar miracles are happening in other parts of the world. Let's move along to Exhibit C.

From Dead Religion to Missionary Zeal

This portion of the world is a continent which has gone through some amazing changes in the past one hundred years. Let's talk about the entire continent first, and then focus on one of its nations.

This area of the world has been chronically poor and known for human exploitation. Compared to another continent in the same hemisphere two hundred years ago, this region of focus had twice as many slaves that lived in far worse conditions than its wealthier neighbor. Yet that neighbor is often historically portrayed as the greatest exploiter of slavery.[10]

In 1900, if you'd taken the spiritual pulse of this region, you might have been disturbed by the result. Many people were nominally religious, but it was of the lukewarm or dead variety. Most people didn't attend regular worship, and if you'd asked them then if they knew Jesus personally or were born again, only about fifty thousand would have said yes.

Today over *one hundred million* of the people of Latin America say "Sí!" And many of them are Pentecostals who have a great heart for evangelism and missions.[11]

The people of Latin America have powerfully come to life in the past few generations. In some nations the evangelical population is approaching 40 percent. Latin America used to be a poor, undeveloped, nominally Catholic region of the world. Today a number of nations are taking their place in world missions.

A major case in point is Brazil, the country alluded to earlier that had twice as many slaves as the United States. Once considered a country with one of the largest missionary fields—the Amazon Basin—today Brazil has become the second largest missionary-sending nation in the world.[12] *Brasileros* have set their sights on reaching hundreds of unreached peoples around the world—including many in Muslim nations. A personal story will illustrate their growing impact.

I was leading a mission outreach in Albania in 1991, just two years after the fall of the Iron Curtain. Albania was a Muslim-dominated nation for four hundred years prior to seven decades of ruthless communism. It was the world's first professed atheist nation. When we arrived in the country, 70 percent of the men were unemployed, and commerce was nonexistent. We stayed with a woman who had worn the same dress for twenty years. Yet God was beginning to move in people's hearts.

One day we were invited to share the good news in a village in the mountains where our hosts said no Christians had ever ministered (at least in the past five hundred years). Our team was excited to share God's love in this virgin territory. However, when we arrived, we found a team of Brazilians actively engaged in planting a church! We excitedly joined their pioneer efforts.

A fresh wind is blowing across much of Latin America. Brazilians are ministering worldwide; Argentina has experienced revival, resulting in some of the largest churches in the world. A dead or sleepy continent is now brimming with missional zeal. *Latin Americans will be a part of the Fourth Wave.*

But wait! There's another amazing display across the room that tells the story of a different continent and nation. Please take the time to visit Exhibit D.

From Prayer Target to Prayer Leader

This vast region of the world was almost entirely isolated from the gospel for thousands of years. Some facts were known from history about the peoples of the north, but nearly nothing of those that populated the central and southern regions.

Then a bold, adventurous chap, who became the nineteenth century's most recognizable celebrity, undertook some amazing explorations of these mysterious lands and opened them up for the world. His books became instant best-sellers and put this resource-laden region into the hearts and prayers of millions. Soon, missionaries began to travel to this huge continent to share the love of Christ.

I don't think any other continent has been a greater object of prayer than Africa, which opened up to Christian missions through David Livingstone's nineteenth-century adventures (we will discuss his Second Wave impact in chapter 6). However, in the twenty-first century, those who have been prayed *for* are becoming the prayer leaders *of* the world. Here's the story of how one nation, South Africa—the land of apartheid—became the land of repentance and prayer.

In July 2000 God captured the heart of a South African businessman, Graham Power, with a vision based on 2 Chronicles 7:14. That following March, more than 45,000 believers united for a Day of Repentance and Prayer at a rugby stadium in Cape Town. It was a day of intense intercession that caused the vision of prayer to spread into the rest of South Africa.

In February 2002 Graham Power had a second vision. The whole of Africa was to gather in a Day of Repentance and Prayer, changing Africa to become a "light to the world." Eventually, Africa was to invite all the nations of the globe to unite in this move of transformational intercession.

On May 2, 2004, history was made when Christians from all fifty-six African nations participated in the first ever continental Day of Repentance and Prayer for Africa. Numerous communities, villages, towns, and cities united in prayer gatherings. In the nation of South Africa, 277 communities participated.

The Global Day of Prayer—birthed in Africa and led by Africans—now unites Christians from over 220 countries every May to cry out to God. It is the largest prayer movement in the history of the world.[13] Africa was once the prayer focus of the developed nations. Now the continent of Africa is leading the world in fervent, repentant intercession. *Africans will be a part of the Fourth Wave.*

We have one final stop on our global missions tour—Exhibit E.

From Warrior to Peace Ambassador

There is a group of nations in the world that have been extremely resistant to the good news of Jesus Christ. This religious bloc has an uneven past that includes both literary and technical achievements (eighth to thirteenth centuries) and totalitarian control, grueling poverty, and abuse of human rights. Some of its extreme adherents want to subjugate the world through a violent holy war called *jihad.*

This group of over forty nations located from North Africa to the Middle East, from Central Asia to Indonesia, is known as the Muslim World.

It was into this world that Mosab Hassan Yousef was born in 1978, in Ramallah, Palestine, six miles north of Jerusalem. Mosab's father, Sheikh

Hassan Yousef, was a founder of Hamas (an acronym for the Arabic words "Islamic Resistance Movement"), considered by the European Union, Israel, Japan, Canada, and the United States to be a terrorist organization.

When Mosab was growing up, he wanted to be a fighter because that was expected of Arab children in the West Bank. He was first arrested when he was ten, during the First Intifada, for throwing rocks at Israeli settlers. He was arrested and jailed by the Israelis numerous times. As his father's eldest son, he was seen as the heir apparent and became an important part of the Hamas organization.

Yousef was jailed by the Israel Security Agency (ISA) in 1996. During this time, he says he learned of the severe forms of torture used by Hamas. That's when he began to doubt the validity of jihad—especially rationalizing the suffering of innocent people during attacks. Soon Yousef's faith in militant Islam was shattered, and he determined to become an Israeli informant.

After his release from prison in 1997, Yousef was considered Israel's most reliable source in the Hamas leadership. The information Yousef gave to Israeli intelligence exposed a number of Hamas cells and plots. As a result, dozens of suicide bombings and assassination attempts on Israeli figures were thwarted, including a plan to assassinate President Shimon Peres.

In 1999 Yousef met a British missionary who introduced him to the love of Jesus Christ. After a year of soul-searching, Yousef gave his life to Jesus (*Isa* in the Arabic language), was baptized, and in 2007 moved to the United States, where he continues to grow in his faith.[14]

Yousef's heart's desire today is to bring peace to the Middle East through the Prince of Peace. He's not alone. Christians ministering quietly in the Middle East say Muslims are coming to Christ at an unprecedented rate. Tom Doyle, the Middle East–Central Asia director for e3 Partners, says, "Probably in the last ten years, more Muslims have come to faith in Christ than in the last fifteen centuries of Islam."[15] In the summer of 2010, two hundred former Muslims were baptized during a training conference in Europe led by Iran-born evangelist Lazarus Yeghnazar. Muslims have had miraculous visitations and revelations of Jesus in a number of nations in recent years.[16] In Iran, an underground movement of house churches has sprung up, involving thousands of believers in Jesus.[17] *Muslim-background believers (MBBs) will be a part of the Fourth Wave.*

Changes Ahead

As we've seen, vast movements to Christ are taking place in many parts of the world. The makeup of the church is shifting geographically. The application of faith in family life, business, politics, and many aspects of culture is an astounding twenty-first-century sea change. But the greatest changes are still ahead.

What could happen in the coming years? Will we see

- millions of Messianic Muslims involved in global missions,
- ten million Chinese missionaries and a Chinese church on every corner,
- increased growth of Islam in Europe or the re-evangelization of the continent by its former colonies,
- the collapse or renewal of the United States,
- a one-world government in some shape or form?

Only God knows, and he never tells.[18]

What we do know is that a fourth wave of modern missions has begun, and it will have a major bearing on all these questions. There's a task to be done, and its accomplishment will greatly affect the next chapter of history.

So to history we turn, where God has launched many missional waves over the past five thousand years. Here's an important idea to keep in mind: *your view of history greatly determines how you live your life.*

Chapter 2

Ancient Waves

IF YOU ARE HINDU and believe that history is cyclical, you will most likely not improve your circumstances but simply live for survival. (This worldview is partly responsible for the vast poverty in India.) If you are a communist and believe that history is moving toward a collectivist utopia, you will work to bring a revolution to achieve the goal. (Think communist China and Cuba). If you are a fundamentalist Muslim, you may try to create as much chaos in the world as you can to bring *sharia* law to every nation with the goal of ushering in the final triumph of Islam. (Does Iran or Saudi Arabia come to mind?) If you are secular in outlook, you will most likely live for the "here and now" without an eye on eternity. (We see this among many in America and Europe).

The Bible presents a linear view of history. God is the Author and Finisher of the human drama and is directing the affairs of men toward an ultimate conclusion that centers around the lordship of Jesus Christ. Believers have a task to do in this march of history—to "go into all the world and preach the Good News to everyone" (Mark 16:15). Bringing the message of salvation and the teachings of Jesus to every person and nation will bring many blessings to human culture and society and prepare the way for an eternal kingdom of love and light.

The student of the Bible and of history also knows that this forward thrust of the good news has taken place in waves over thousands of years. My earliest encounter with Christian missions was all about waves—waves of young people coming up on the shores of the world.

In 1972 I had traveled to New Zealand to find God. Not that I felt he lived there exclusively, but rather a door had opened for me and three other young collegians to take a break from our studies and travel halfway around the world to be discipled, engage in evangelism, and grow in our young faith.

Loren Cunningham, the founder of Youth With A Mission, was speaking at the podium of the YMCA in Auckland that October. He, along with Don Stephens, now CEO of Mercy Ships, and Brother Andrew, founder of Open Doors, were on a worldwide missions recruiting tour following YWAM's first Olympic Games outreach in Munich, Germany. The Olympic venue had been scarred by the terrorist assassination of eight Israeli athletes. YWAMers and other believers had taken to the streets of Munich to share roses and prayers with the shaken populace in a powerful display of love and reconciliation.

Loren was sharing a vision that God had given him in 1959. He said God had shown him that waves of youth would be coming to the shores of all the continents of the world, sharing their faith.[1] It was a great visual. I could see the "waves" in my mind's eye, crashing on the beaches, and thought it was cool that young people were the focus. I didn't realize at the time that youth had never before been significantly involved in world evangelism. When Loren gave the missions altar call, I was one of the first to get up out of my seat and make my way to the front. I asked the three men where I could sign up.

Something—rather, Someone—was stirring in my heart, calling me to join the waves of young people who were coming to every nation on earth.

That initial encounter took me to Europe, then Africa, then the Americas, then finally Asia. Over four decades I came to realize that the loving God of the universe has been launching waves of redemption for thousands of years. Some of those waves of salvation were very ancient indeed.

One Mission since the Fall

Have you ever wondered why the Old Testament portion of the Bible is twice as large as the New Testament? Its content includes a description of our origins, prophetic books, poetry, genealogical lists, and a lot of warfare between peoples and nations.

But that's not the main emphasis. The history of the ancient world is God's story of salvation revealed in many stages, or waves. It is upon this history that our modern world rests. Though some of us tend to shy away from reading the Old Testament, I believe God caused it to be twice as big as the New Testament because he knew its stories, lessons, principles, and foundations were crucial to his plans in history.

Since the fall of humankind in the Garden of Eden, the central focus on earth has been *how* to bring salvation to a race of rebels and God-deniers. Ancient world history as revealed in the Old Testament gives us many clues concerning God's means and methods of bringing people back into relationship with him.

We need to fall in love with the Old Testament narrative again. It contains powerful and awe-inspiring waves of salvation.

Noah and the Flood (Genesis 6–9)

The first major wave of salvation we find in ancient history contained the biggest literal waves to ever hit the earth. It was called *the Flood*. Its primary purpose was to reveal the broken heart of God over man's rebellion and to judge the earth for its sins (Genesis 6). This was a wave of judgment. But eight people—Noah's family—got up on top of that wave by faith and were saved from the cataclysmic changes that came to the entire earth. Noah and his family helped begin the world anew because they believed and obeyed.

We might call it the "Flood Revival," with only eight people being saved. Noah and his family were rescued because he found favor in the eyes of the Lord (Gen. 6:8), he walked with God (Gen. 6:9), and was a preacher of righteousness (2 Pet. 2:5). We will see these same characteristics in many future missionary leaders.

Abraham and the Nation of Israel (Genesis 12–25)

The next major step in God's salvation waves took place around 2000 BC when God found a man in Ur named Abram. The Lord called him out of his ancestral country to go to a new land, taught him faith and friendship, and severely tested him. When he passed the test, God changed his name to Abraham, and promised: "Because you have obeyed me and have not withheld even your son, your only son, I swear by my own name that I will certainly bless you. I will multiply your descendants beyond number, like the stars in the sky and the sand on the seashore. Your descendants will conquer the cities of their enemies. And through your descendants all the nations of the earth will be blessed" (Gen. 22:16–18).

The Abrahamic covenant, seemingly a ripple in God's vast ocean tide of salvation, continued through son Isaac, grandson Jacob, and then lay dormant in slavery in Egypt for four hundred years. It would take a man whose name means "drawn out of the waters" to launch the next big wave of Old Testament salvation.

Moses and the Exodus (Exodus 1–15)

Some of us can relate to Moses. He was a bashful, reluctant servant of God—a man who took things into his own hands, killed an Egyptian, and almost destroyed his God-given destiny. It was only after forty years of out-of-state "Desert Bible School" that Moses once again encountered I AM WHO I AM and reluctantly agreed to lead the next ancient wave of salvation.

That wave, *the Exodus*, brought up to two million people out of Egypt after a display of God's power and the impotence of the Egyptians' idols. The literal waves in this harrowing narrative defied the powers of nature. To allow the children of Israel to escape from Pharaoh and his hordes, God caused the waters of the Red Sea to stand up on both sides—a reverse wave!—allowing the Israelites to escape. Then he ordered the waves to perform their natural function—crashing down and drowning the Egyptians who had sought to keep Israel in slavery.

Thus the nation of Israel was saved, delivered, and established as a redeemed people that day. Soon after, in the same desert place where God had first spoken to Moses from a burning bush, the Lord of salvation gave his moral code—the Ten Commandments—to the people with the expectation that they would live them and share them with the world. They failed the assignment, but the forming and establishing of Israel as a covenant nation was the single greatest launching pad of all subsequent waves of salvation. It would eventually lead to the coming of the Messiah-Savior Jesus Christ and to all the resulting waves of outreach we will discuss in future chapters.

That tiny nation of Israel is still central in world history, making headlines almost daily. Another wave of salvation is yet to come to modern Jews through which "all Israel will be saved" (Rom. 11:26).

Before we discuss that providential day, let's highlight other waves of salvation that are recorded in Old Testament history. These were seasons of prayer, renewal, dedication, and consecration of large numbers of people who turned to the Lord in their respective generations. They serve as primers for what God will do in our own time.

Israel's Waves of Renewal . . . and Decline

It's fascinating to read the story of Israel's national history in 1 and 2 Samuel, 1 and 2 Kings, 1 and 2 Chronicles, and other Old Testament books. They reveal the commonality of the cycles of life in a fallen world. Many of our cultures and nations—especially those that have heard the message of the gospel—go through similar seasons of revival and blessing, disobedience and decline. These stories are peppered with leaders and people that loved God with their whole hearts, with half a heart, or those who were essentially heartless. This matches our experience with human nature, even in some of our own acquaintances and families.

In this section we will highlight six different waves of renewal or salvation that were experienced during Israel's corporate history. Keep two truths in mind as you ponder these stories. One is that *those who don't know history are condemned to repeat it.* The other is that *he who walks with wise men will be wise* (Prov. 13:20 NKJV).

If we choose the latter lesson rather than the former, God can use us in this generation to be agents of salvation in many lives.

David (1 Samuel 16 to 1 Kings 2)

Israel's second king, David, the sweet psalmist of Israel, who killed the giant Goliath because of his courageous faith in God, was instrumental in uniting the Jews in 1010 BC. This historical account provides a vivid image of the Messiah Jesus, who is referred to in Scripture as the Son of David (Matt. 21:9). David was a "man after God's own heart" (Acts 13:22), who established celebratory worship in the kingdom and governed in righteousness and the fear of the Lord. He had his faults and sins (especially his adultery with Bathsheba and having her husband, Uriah, killed in battle), but his love for God brought unity and a renewal of worship throughout the kingdom (e.g., 1 Chron. 15, 16). His vision and preparations for the temple brought God's salvation plan out into the open (1 Chron. 22). We need to have the *heart* of David.

Solomon (1 Chronicles 28 to 2 Chronicles 10)

David's son by Bathsheba, Solomon, Israel's third king, reigned around 970 BC. Solomon was given great riches and wisdom from God because of his early humility and commitment to the Lord. It was Solomon who completed the building of the magnificent temple and ushered in the Golden Age of the Jewish nation. Upon dedicating the temple to God's service, the *shekinah* glory fell on the priests and people. God so blessed the early years of Solomon that gold was plentiful in the kingdom, and silver was considered common! Solomon celebrated a great Passover feast with thousands of sacrifices to the Lord. Unfortunately, over his lifetime, Solomon allowed his many wives to turn his heart away from God's service (1 Kings 11:4). Nevertheless, we need to strive to become *wise* like Solomon was in his youth.

Asa (2 Chronicles 14–16)

Asa was Israel's fifth king—the third to serve in Judah after the kingdom was divided between north and south. Asa was loyal to God most of his life and was used by God to cleanse the land of immorality and idol worship after a time of decline. Under his leadership there was a national revival where the nation "entered into a covenant to seek the Lord, the God of their ancestors, with all their heart and soul" (2 Chron. 15:12). God specifically used King Asa to clean up the immoral, sexually idolatrous lives of the people. We need to have a desire for *sexual purity* like King Asa. This call to holiness or personal purity will be seen in many future awakenings of God's people in history.

Jehoshaphat (2 Chronicles 17–20)

King Jehoshaphat, Asa's son, followed his father's faith. Around 860 BC he established teaching circuits throughout the nation where priests would travel to train and equip the people (2 Chron. 17:7–9). These teaching circuits would later surface during the Methodist Revival with their famous circuit riders. Jehoshaphat "took delight in the ways of the Lord; moreover he removed the high places and wooden images from Judah" (17:6–7 NKJV). He had a joyous passion for God and a hatred of sin and its effects. We need to understand the importance of *good teaching* (discipleship) as did King Jehoshaphat.

Hezekiah (2 Chronicles 29–32)

Some one hundred and fifty years after the rule of Jehoshaphat, around 715 BC, the nation of Israel once again turned from God and followed the ways of the world. God's next wave of Old Testament salvation and renewal took place through a twenty-five-year-old king named Hezekiah. His father, Ahaz, had been one of the more wicked leaders of the kingdom. Hezekiah rejected his father's bad example, and followed the example of righteous leaders. He restored the temple and the Passover feast, and according to Scripture, "in all that he did in the service of the Temple of God and in his efforts to follow God's laws, Hezekiah sought his God wholeheartedly. As a result, he was very successful" (2 Chron. 31:21). We need to be *obedient* to God, like King Hezekiah.

Josiah (2 Kings 22–23 and 2 Chronicles 34–35)

We will finish our discussion of ancient waves of salvation (missions) with a more in-depth look into one of the latter kings of Judah, who was also its greatest. How would you like this inscription on your own tombstone: "Never before had there been a king like Josiah, who turned to the Lord with all his heart and soul and strength, obeying all the laws of Moses. And there has never been a king like him since" (2 Kings 23:25).

What a life! There were none greater before him (including David, Solomon, Asa, Jehoshaphat, and Hezekiah) and none greater after him.

Let's take a closer look at this Old Testament "missional king" who was used by God to bring a national revival to the southern kingdom of Judah. How did he do it? What principles in his life can we apply to our efforts today?

The story of national renewal under King Josiah is found in 2 Kings 23 and 2 Chronicles 34. Josiah enters the historical narrative around 640 BC, the grandson of wicked King Manasseh and son of his short-lived, worldly father, Amon, who died at age twenty-four. Josiah ascends the throne at eight years of age. Coming from a dysfunctional family during a time of judgment and decline in the kingdom, one would expect that his rule would be similar and short-lived. However, Josiah, even at an early age, showed a greatness of character that allowed him to bring a nation back into relationship with God.

How did the boy-king do it? There were eight principles in his life that will reappear in future missionary leaders and movements. Let's learn them well.

First, *he was committed to a righteous lifestyle*. He "did what was right in the sight of the Lord and walked in the ways of his father David; he did not turn aside to the right hand or to the left" (2 Chron. 34:2 NKJV). That wasn't easy to do for an eight-year-old from a bad family! Yet he rejected their example and followed the memory of the great King David. A missional life always begins with a commitment to do right, no matter your background, circumstances, pressures, or temptations. Josiah had tunnel vision for doing what was right for the glory of God.

Second, *he was committed to prayer.* "In the eighth year of his reign, while he was still young, he began to seek the God of his father David" (2 Chron. 34:3 NKJV). "Seeking God" in biblical language means developing your prayer life, something Josiah did by the age of sixteen. Prayer is the fuel of missions, which we will discover again in many periods of evangelistic outreach. Apparently at an early age, Josiah became a prayer warrior and seeker of God, which brought revelation, understanding, and stability to his life. A strong prayer life is one of the secrets of a missional believer.

Third, *he was committed to warring against sin.* "In the twelfth year [of his reign] he began to purge Judah and Jerusalem of the high places, the wooden images, the carved images, and the molded images . . ." (2 Chron. 34:3–7 NKJV). One of the central ideas that Josiah learned through prayer by the age of twenty is that God hates sin because it destroys human lives and potential. He shared God's burden and grief over idolatrous living, and decided to start a war in the nation against the sin that was rotting its foundations. Because he was king, he tore down idols, burned bones of pagan priests, and undertook many other aggressive acts. I don't encourage you to apply Josiah's methods unless you are the absolute ruler of a kingdom. In our democratic world, those actions will lead you into jail ministry. However, Josiah did what was proper in his time to cleanse the kingdom of its sins. There is no freedom without turning from sin.

Fourth, *he was committed to building up the worship of God.* "In the eighteenth year of his reign, when he had purged the land and the temple, he sent Shaphan the son of Azaliah . . . to repair the house of the Lord his God" (2 Chron. 34:8–13 NKJV). By now this amazingly wise and mature twenty-six-year-old was ready to renew the praise of God in the culture. The temple had been partially destroyed and was apparently not in use. Josiah sent people to clean up and repair the house of God because he knew the people must be pointed to their Savior. Hating sin is not enough. We need to love the worship and service of God and do everything in our power to improve it. In our day it means being committed to the renewal and growth of the church, which is his New Testament temple (2 Cor.

6:16). We need to champion church renewal and corporate worship. Missional followers of Christ are committed to building up the church.

Fifth, *he was committed to reverence for God and his law.* "Thus it happened, when the king heard the words of the Law, that he tore his clothes . . . saying . . . 'great is the wrath of the Lord that is poured out on us, because our fathers have not kept the word of the Lord, to do according to all that is written in this book'" (2 Chron. 34:19–21 NKJV). When the workers were rebuilding the temple, they came across a copy of the Law that had been buried in the rubble. When they brought it to the king, he showed great respect for its words and sent the leaders to prophetically inquire what God's plans were for the nation. What's astounding about this part of the story is that this is the first time Josiah has heard the reading of the Old Testament Bible—the Law. Up to this point he has lived a righteous life, learned to pray, hated sin, and built up worship—all without a Bible. When he hears it for the first time, he shows reverence and awe. Part of our mission must be to show great respect for God and his Word.

Sixth, *he was committed to tender brokenness and humility before God.* "Because your heart was tender and you humbled yourself before God when you heard his words against this place and against its inhabitants, and you humbled yourself before Me and you tore your clothes and wept before Me, I also have heard you, says the Lord" (2 Chron. 34:27 NKJV). To find out God's view of Judah's future, Josiah sent a delegation to the godliest person in the kingdom—a woman named Huldah. (We will see in future chapters the critical role of women, especially today, in global missions.) Huldah, we are told, sends a message back from God that greatly reveals Josiah's heart. God says he is pleased with his humble attitude and tears, so the kingdom will not be judged immediately. Prior to this revelation, one might conclude that Josiah is a macho-man—a Type A personality—that only enjoys warring against sin. These verses reveal the inner heart of Josiah: he is a broken man with a tender heart. Missional leaders share this tenderness of spirit. It keeps them from the imbalance of only hating sin.

But the best of the story is found in the final two principles of his life.

Seventh, *he was committed to God's Word and its importance to the whole of his kingdom.* "Then the king sent and gathered all the elders of

Judah and Jerusalem . . . and the inhabitants of Jerusalem. . . . And he read in their hearing the words of the book of the covenant which had been found in the house of the Lord" (2 Chron. 34:29–30 NKJV). Josiah had heard God's Word and knew it was good for him. What was good for him was also good for every person in his kingdom. So he gathered all the people together—an assembly for the entire capital city—and he *personally* read God's words to the people. There had been other city-wide and national gatherings in Israel's history. But in most of them, it was the priests—the spiritual leaders—that handled the duties of "Bible-reading." Josiah understood that he needed to reinforce the importance of God's Word to the people by reading it himself. He refused to delegate it. Missional believers are also lovers of God's Word who understand that its words and teachings are crucial to the history of nations.[2]

Finally, *he was committed to covenant action with God in thoroughly mobilizing his sphere of influence.* "Then the king stood in his place and made a covenant before the Lord, to follow the Lord, and to keep His commandments and His testimonies and His statutes with all his heart and all his soul. . . . And he made all who were present in Jerusalem and Benjamin take a stand" (2 Chron. 34:31–32 NKJV). From the age of twelve, Josiah was on a mission which grew into the revival of a nation. On this special day, after personally reading the words of God to the people, Josiah publicly committed to follow God wholeheartedly and asked his subjects to follow him. This would be like the president of a nation coming on national television and declaring his desire to follow God and inviting all his fellow citizens to join him. Josiah was a covenant follower—half-baked resolutions were not enough for him. He made a public commitment to God and invited others to join him. He used his influence as king to thoroughly engage his sphere of influence. Missional followers make a covenant with God to use their power and influence to bring as many as possible to salvation.

What's most stunning about this real life story in ancient history is that after Josiah lived out these missional principles, the Bible says that "All his days they did not depart from following the Lord God of their fathers" (2 Chron. 34:33 NKJV).

In other words, they did it! This story begins in 2 Chronicles 34:1 with a nation in ruinous decline, with an eight-year-old king ascending the throne. It ends thirty-two verses and eighteen years later with a nation in major revival. Salvation has come to thousands. God is being honored and followed. That renewal lasted for thirteen years.

Josiah lived up to his name, which means "one who is founded on God (Yahweh)."

Through his faith and obedience, like others in the ancient world, God used Josiah in his generation to bring a wave of salvation to people. Those Old Testament waves eventually died off and lay still for hundreds of years as the nation of Israel and its mandate to bring blessing to the all the nations was stalled.

But another wave—centered on the person of Jesus Christ—was about to begin. We now turn our attention to the amazing story of the Early Church Wave of evangelization that created Christian missions—and changed the course of history.

Chapter 3

The Early Church Wave

FROM ITS INCEPTION, the early church was on a mission. They had walked with Jesus for years. They'd listened to his teachings, experienced his miracles, and watched him die in cruel agony while hanging from a cross. Some had denied him; others were confused and ran away. But after his death and resurrection, they began to understand who he really was—God in the flesh—and grew to accept the mission he had given them.

Jesus himself had set the missional direction for his followers by leaving the comforts of heaven, coming to earth, laying down his life for the sins of all people, and commissioning his disciples to go and do likewise (John 20:21).

During his post-resurrection appearances with his disciples, Jesus gave four clear commands that have summed up the Christian missionary enterprise. The first one, found in Matthew 28:18–20, is often called the *what* of world evangelization: "I have been given all authority in heaven and on earth. Therefore, go and make disciples of all the nations, baptizing them in the name of the Father and the Son and the Holy Spirit. Teach these new disciples to obey all the commands I have given you. And be sure of this: I am with you always, even to the end of the age." Leslie Lyall of Overseas Missionary Fellowship says that by Jesus' death and resurrection, he defeated the great usurper and was soon to charge his church to possess his possessions and to enter into his heritage.[1]

Secondly, Jesus describes the *where* of the Christian mission: "Go into all the world and preach the Good News to everyone" (Mark 16:15). This is the founding verse of YWAM that was given to Loren Cunningham while seeing a vision of waves of young people coming to the shores of the world in 1959.[2]

The third axiom of the call is the *when* of world missions. When Jesus suddenly appeared to the disciples in Jerusalem after he had met two of them on the road to Emmaus, he told them that in the authority of his name,

> this message would be proclaimed . . . to all the nations, beginning in Jerusalem: "There is forgiveness of sins for all who repent." You are witnesses of all these things.
>
> And now I will send the Holy Spirit, just as my Father promised. But stay here in the city until the Holy Spirit comes and fills you with power from heaven. (Luke 24:47–49)

The early followers of Jesus were to wait for an important infilling of the Holy Spirit in the Jewish capital city and then take the message of God's love and forgiveness to every nation on earth.

Finally, there is the *how* of the missional enterprise, found in Acts 1:8. Jesus said, "But you will receive power when the Holy Spirit comes upon you. And you will be my witnesses, telling people about me everywhere—in Jerusalem, throughout Judea, in Samaria, and to the ends of the earth."

Thus the comprehensive nature of missions is that God has called his people to make disciples of all the nations—demonstrating their changed lives through baptism and growing by teaching others. He has commanded us to take the message of his love and forgiveness to every person in every part of the world. He asked his early followers to wait to begin that mission until they had received a supernatural empowerment from the Holy Spirit, the third person of the Trinity. Then, in the power of the Holy Spirit, they were to go global—starting where they were, going to regions nearby, and eventually filling the entire world with the message of God's love.

As we've seen from our brief tour of ancient history, the plan of salvation began a long time ago. J. Herbert Kane in his classic work *Christian Missions in Biblical Perspective* writes:

> The Christian mission is a part of God's sovereign activity in the realm of redemption. From first to last the Christian mission is God's mission, not man's. It originated in the heart of God. It is based on the love of God. It is determined by the will of God. Its mandate was enunciated by the Son of God. Its rationale is explained in the Word of God. For its ultimate success, it is dependent on the power of God. Nowhere is the sovereignty of God more clearly seen than in the Christian mission.[3]

Pentecost Revival!

The early church obeyed the commands of Jesus and spent ten days praying about their assignment in an upper room in Jerusalem. They confessed their sins to one another—especially the eleven who had abandoned Jesus the night of his arrest, most notably Peter who cowardly betrayed his Lord. They recounted the years Jesus had walked with them, taught them about the kingdom of God, addressed their deepest needs, healed the sick, and raised the dead. Then they passionately prayed to God to give them the grace and ability to do what he was asking them to do.

Ten days after Jesus' ascension into heaven, God poured out his Spirit on the day of Pentecost (Acts 2:1–4). On that day of the beginning of the Christian mission, 120 people were filled with power by the living God. The disciples flooded out into the streets speaking about God's goodness in various languages they had never learned.

Talk about spiritual shock and awe! Christian historian Kenneth Scott Latourette says that the coming of the Holy Spirit was of major importance because it changed the believers into enthusiastic witnesses.[4]

Dennis Bennett, one of the early leaders of the charismatic renewal, describes the early church mission-launching day this way:

They were praising God, praying, going to the Temple; they even had a business meeting and an election! (Acts 1:15–26) . . . On the Feast of Pentecost, the Feast of the First-Fruits, the power came. . . . He overflowed from them out into the world around, inspiring them to praise and glorify God, not only in their own tongues, but in new languages, and in so doing, tamed their tongues to his use, freed their spirits, renewed their minds, refreshed their bodies, and brought power to witness.[5]

Bennett goes on to describe the reaction of the many visitors who were in Jerusalem at the time for the Feast:

Some jeered and said, "They're just drunk, that's all!" but Peter responded: "No, they're not drunk! After all, it's only 9 o'clock in the morning! But this is that which was prophesied by Joel, 'In the last days, says God, I will pour out my Spirit upon all flesh.'" (Acts 2:13–17). So convincing were the signs that three thousand of those "devout men" accepted Jesus as Messiah, repented of their sins, were baptized, and themselves received the gift of the Holy Spirit that day.[6]

Christian missions—New Testament missions—began on Pentecost, following the death and resurrection of Jesus. Many thousands joined the disciples in the coming years as they proclaimed Christ's message and obeyed the commands of their risen King.

The Acts story also mentions the self-sacrifice and generosity of the early followers as they met the needs of those around them, flowing out of a heart of love for Jesus. The changed lives of the growing church were a magnet of attraction in a dark, dreary, and harsh Roman outpost named Palestine. Jesus had given them eternal hope, and that hope was highly combustible through a godly mix of revival fire. Over the next seventy years, the early church would grow into hundreds of thousands of followers of Jesus the Messiah.

There were at least three keys to missional success during the time of the early church as recorded in Acts:

- *Revival!*—on the day of Pentecost (Acts 2:1–40)
- *Prayer*—in the upper room and the temple, which preceded the outpouring of God's Spirit (Acts 1:13; 2:1)
- *Unity*—as seen in their love for each other (Acts 2:44–46)

These three keys helped bring multitudes to Christ during the early church era (e.g., Acts 2:41, 42, 47). Two other elements also played strategic roles. One is *providence,* which relates to God's choice of missionaries, timing, and his sovereign actions in each period in history. The other is *technology,* or the civilization developments that aided each missions advance. We will look in depth at these five factors in chapter 4.

But first let's introduce the importance of God's providence and technology in the rise of the Early Church Wave.

Providence and the Early Church

God himself chose the time in history and the specific place for Jesus to come to earth to launch the redemption of the world (Gal. 4:4). Jesus shared the good news with the Jewish race almost exclusively (Matt. 15:24), and his first followers were Jews. As such, the first New Testament thrust in missions was Jewish-led by God's sovereign choice and centered in Jerusalem. When Jewish believers were slow in taking the message to Judea and Samaria, God allowed persecution to spring up, which scattered the early believers in those directions (Acts 8). During this time period, Peter received the vision of the gospel going to the non-Jewish people (Acts 10), and Saul, later named Paul, was led by God to become the apostle to the Gentiles (Gal. 2:7).

After these events, God gave clear instructions on the trajectory of global missions. Following prayer and the laying on of hands (Acts 13:3), Paul launched the church's first recorded missionary journeys. On Paul's second trip, the Holy Spirit specifically forbade him from taking the good news east into Asia Minor. Instead, through the Macedonian call (see Acts 16:6–13), God told Paul to pioneer and plant churches in the west—which would set the pattern and primary direction of world evangelization for the next two thousand years. E. Glenn Hinson believes that the principal strategy for the expansion of Christianity was to plant churches which could continue to attract and enlist converts. This network of fellowships, strongly committed to hospitality, provided a transportation system for missionaries.[7]

The Roman Empire, which extended from northern Africa to the far reaches of Great Britain and eastward to the Caspian Sea, had been prepared for the next step in the plan of world evangelization. Both blacks and whites would be commissioned as messengers of the good news in the Roman world. Jewish settlements already dotted the empire, and they would be the most effective depots for further dispersion of God's grace and as jumping-off points into Gentile communities. Hinson goes on to explain:

> The immense success of Christianity in penetrating the Graeco-Roman Empire and its accommodation to Hellenistic culture within so short a span of time can be explained only on the assumption of the extensive preliminary preparation by Hellenistic Judaism. There can be no question that at the beginning of the Christian era, Judaism was an ardently missionary faith which "compassed land and sea" to make proselytes. It had already tilled the vast field of the Empire as a preparation for the Christian Gospel.[8]

Revival fires of the early church swept through already-plowed fields, which eventually sprouted seeds throughout the entire Roman Empire.

Technology

Other cultural and civilization factors were critical to missional advance in the early centuries—most of them created by the *Pax Romana*, the Roman Peace, which dominated the known world. Greek and Roman civilization had combined to build a vast system of roads throughout the empire that encouraged travel, trade, and cultural exchange. There was also the "universality" and accuracy of the Greek language, which served as a perfect vehicle for the dissemination of the gospel.

Historian Harold R. Cook believes that political unification under Roman rule, the network of roads, use of sea lanes, and the widespread use of the Greek language favored the spread of the new faith.[9] Michael Pocock has written that people migrations were also crucial to Christianity's expansion in the first five centuries AD.[10]

Thus, a unified and relatively open civilization, large-scale migrations, a great network of roads, and a precise, universally used language were God's cultural tools during the early advance of Christian missions. Initially Jews led the gospel advance, but soon the Gentile peoples living throughout the Roman Empire began turning to Christ and engaging in the mission. University of Texas professor Rodney Stark states in his work *Discovering God* that by AD 350 the Christian population of the empire numbered many millions.[11]

Birthed in revival, fueled by prayer and unity, directed by God's providence, and using the most advanced developments and technologies of the era, the first wave of Christian missions had spread west and north throughout the reaches of the Roman Empire—eventually leading approximately half of its population to faith in Christ.[12] J. Herbert Kane describes the next stage in Christian missions:

> Following the conversion of Constantine, Christianity entered a period of unprecedented expansion. During the fourth century, the number of Christians multiplied by some 400 percent. Between AD 500 and 1200, Christian missionaries—many of them monks— roamed all over Europe teaching and preaching the gospel and establishing monasteries which became centers of not only light and learning but also of missionary activity. . . . Christianity then spread far beyond the borders of the Roman Empire.[13]

The growth of the Christian faith, even during the chaotic days of the Middle Ages, was changing the face of the civilized world and laying the foundation for further developments in Europe and beyond. Missionaries had also arrived in the Far East—starting centuries earlier with the apostle Thomas in India. An ancient missionary movement called the

Nestorians had reached all the way into what is now China as early as AD 635.[14]

However, it was not until the eighteenth century that a rebirth of global missions vision would be fully realized—and this "gospel of the kingdom" would be catapulted into every nation on earth.

But before we go there, let's examine the missional factors in every generation that are crucial for God's rising tide of salvation.

Chapter 4

What Causes Rising Tides?

Since nature reveals the Creator in marvelous ways, it is helpful to compare missionary surges with rising tides and ocean swells. Weather phenomena such as storms produce swells, which in turn produce waves. Tides affect the shape of the waves—either steeper at low tide or "mushier" at high tide.

We know many things about physical tides. They are a complex gravitational reaction between the moon, sun, and earth.

- The gravitational force of the moon is one ten-millionth that of earth, but when you combine other forces, such as the earth's centrifugal force created by its spin, you get tides.
- The sun's gravitational force on the earth is only 46 percent that of the moon; thus, the moon is the single most important factor for the creation of tides.
- The sun's gravity also produces tides. But since the forces are smaller, as compared to the moon, the effects are greatly decreased.
- Tides are not caused by the direct pull of the moon's gravity. The

moon pulls upward on the water, while the earth is pulling downward. There is a slight advantage to the moon, and thus we have tides.[1]

Using creation as a model, God is the moon (the most important factor) in the rising tide of missions; historical situations are the sun (a lesser but important factor); and human wills are the earth (what God is acting upon). When God pulls us toward his purposes in salvation, with historical circumstances being opportune and human beings responding in faith and action, then the tide of global missions starts to rise and waves of outreach are the result.

Here's another way of looking at it.

I live in a part of the world—Puget Sound in the state of Washington—where tides and currents have a great impact on weather, topography, and the flow of life. In fact, Washington has one of the longest sea-water coastlines of all the lower forty-eight states. Our lives are centered around water and the ocean tides.

Currents and tides make a difference. The state of Maine, at the northeastern tip of the United States, sits at approximately the same latitude as the state of Washington, which is located in the northwest corner of the nation. One summer I was visiting Maine, expecting it to be similar in weather to the Pacific Northwest. Not a chance!

During the summertime, the state of Maine and most of the northeastern seaboard states are hot and humid—with temperatures in the 90s and 100s and humidity above 70 percent. This is due to the fact that the Atlantic Ocean current is warm in the summer, allowing hotter temperatures to prevail. In the wintertime, the Atlantic current is cold, bringing temperatures well below zero along with much ice and snow.

On the west coast, Washington has a temperate climate—it's pleasant, with low humidity in the summer and mild temperatures in the winter. The reason for this is that the current of the Pacific Ocean stays 55 degrees all year long, warming the temperatures in the winter and cooling them in the summer.

You can't judge a state by its latitude. You must understand the underlying "currents."

We've mentioned the dynamic nature of tidal activity. Every newspaper in western Washington prints tide tables so that you know when you can fish, clam, and walk the beach, and also when ferries are available. If you don't read the tide tables, you may not understand what's happening around you.

The same thing can be said about the history of missions. I've read many books on missions and many biographies of missionary leaders. Most of them do a good job of sharing the life and times of the person involved. But too often they overlook the spiritual currents and rising tides that greatly impacted the missionary efforts of a given era. Missional outreach never occurs in isolation. It is a combination of God's providential hand acting in history appropriate to the time and circumstances with those who respond to his call.

We have already seen the five factors that influence the rising tide of missions in world history:

- *Revival!*
- *Prayer*
- *Unity*
- *Providence*
- *Technology*

In this chapter we will analyze each of these "undercurrent" elements in God's kingdom enterprise and then, in subsequent chapters, highlight them in each time period. God has amazing methods for impacting the lives of people and nations—and his plans begin with reviving the human heart.

Revival!—The Fire of Missions

I put an exclamation point after the word *revival* to emphasize its dynamic power to change lives. I've experienced personal revival and believe it is at the center of God's calling on my life. I have studied many of the great revivals in history and am amazed how God can ignite the hearts of people who will carry his burden, vision, and passion. He lovingly uses them to change whole nations. I have seen revival fires in various parts of the world, both as an observer and in the role of a revivalist.[2]

The reality we call *revival, spiritual awakening,* or *renewal* can be defined in a variety of ways. (I will use these terms synonymously, though distinctions can be argued.) Here are a few definitions from leading authorities on the subject:

- "Revival is the Church falling in love with Jesus all over again." (Vance Havner)
- "Revival is a community saturated with God." (Duncan Campbell)
- "A revival means days of heaven on earth." (D. Martyn Lloyd-Jones)
- "Revival is God purifying his church." (Erwin Lutzer)
- "Revival is ultimately Christ Himself, seen, felt, heard, living, active, moving in and through His Body on earth." (Stephen Olford)
- "Revival is that strange and sovereign work of God in which he visits his own people, restoring, re-animating, and releasing them into the fullness of his blessings." (Robert Coleman).
- "Revival is a sudden bestowment of a spirit of worship upon God's people." (A. W. Tozer)
- "A true revival means nothing less than a revolution, casting out the spirit of worldliness and selfishness, and making God and His love triumph in the heart and life." (Andrew Murray)
- "Revival is the reformation of the Church for action." (Max Warren)
- "Revival is God revealing Himself to man in awful holiness and irresistible power. It is God's method to counteract spiritual decline and to create spiritual momentum in order that His redemptive purposes might be accomplished on earth." (Arthur Wallis)[3]
- "A revival is nothing else than a new beginning of obedience to God." (Charles Finney)[4]

I personally define historical revival as an awakening of God's people that launches a thrust of evangelism among the lost which results in moral changes in the society.

The word *revival* means "living again." Since Jesus is the way, the truth, and the *life* (John 14:6), revival is Jesus bringing his life in new and powerful ways to his followers. Together with other believers, this revival fire can spread to whole communities, cities, and nations.

All major missionary outreaches are the result of revival breaking out in the hearts of God's people. God reveals his presence, people respond in repentance and faith, and a tide of activity for Christ and his kingdom is born.

As we discuss various waves of Christian missions in subsequent chapters, keep in mind that revived hearts and minds were most likely the original source of the wave of salvation.

Revival is the life of Jesus exploding into missions.

Prayer—The Fuel of Revival

If revival is the fire of missions, then prayer is undoubtedly the fuel of that fire.

Prayer has always been the dynamo of Christian missions. Jesus himself set the standard when he began his ministry with forty days of fasting and prayer. Afterward he returned in the power of the Holy Spirit, and people flocked to his message (Matt. 4:1–25). Later Jesus chose twelve apostles after a night of prayer, and sent them out to share the good news (Luke 6:12–16; 9:1–6). In Matthew 9:37–38 we see Jesus engaged in mission activity in various towns, and it made his heart ache and caused him to exclaim, "What a huge harvest! . . . How few workers!" He then announced the key to future missions success: "On your knees and pray for harvest hands!" (*The Message*).

God invites us to "partner with his providence" through the vehicle of prayer. Through prayer, people's lives are changed. It might be said both from Scripture and experience that *prayer moves the heart and hand of God to act in someone's life* (2 Kings 20:1–11; James 5:13–18). Prayer fuels the redemptive work of the Holy Spirit. As our hearts ache over lost individuals and nations as Jesus' did, we will fall to our knees and pray to the Lord of the harvest. His answer will be to multiply workers (missions) around the world.

As we have seen, the early church fueled its missions outreach by prayer, beginning with a ten-day prayer meeting and confession time in the Upper Room that brought the fire of the Holy Spirit on Pentecost. Peter preached, and thousands were saved (Acts 2:1–41).[5] The disciples continued to pray, and daily people were added to the church (Acts 2:47). In Acts 4:23–30, Luke records a corporate prayer of the early believers where "the place where they were assembled together was shaken; and they were all filled with the Holy Spirit, and they spoke the word of God with boldness" (Acts 4:31 NKJV). There's the success equation: *People pray, the Holy Spirit comes, and powerful outreach takes place.* The U.S. Center for World Mission estimates that prayer-fueled missions brought the ratio of unbelievers to believers in the world to 360:1 by AD 100.[6]

During the Middles Ages, the power of the church greatly impacted the areas of the former Roman Empire and later multiplied throughout Europe through numerous monastic orders where a life devoted to prayer and Bible-reading eventually became the center of medieval society.[7] From Anthony in Egypt (AD 250–350) to Patrick in Ireland to the Nestorians in China and eventually the Franciscans, Dominicans, and Jesuits traveling the globe (twelfth century onward), men and women of God began to fervently pray against the evils of their time while earnestly sharing their faith. They had different burdens and espoused various creeds, but their common denominator was a life devoted to prayer. God honored their efforts, and much of Europe was Christianized as a result— bringing the global unbelievers-to-professing-Christians ratio to 69:1 by AD 1500 at the dawn of the Reformation.[8]

In chapter 5 we will see that following the renewal of the church under Martin Luther, John Calvin, and others, Protestant missions emerged through a young nobleman named Nikolaus von Zinzendorf, who established a community for persecuted believers from Moravia (present-day Czech Republic). After years of turbulent growth, God visited the three-hundred-member Moravian community in revival showers that gave birth to a twenty-four-hour prayer initiative at the village of Herrnhut.

This fervent prayer meeting continued for over one hundred years and launched the first Moravian missionaries into Scandinavia, other parts of Europe, the West Indies, and around the world.[9] It was through a Moravian missionary named Peter Buehler that John Wesley found salvation in Christ and launched the Methodist Revival in England—all of it fueled by prayer.[10]

Many movements of prayer will be evident as we examine each subsequent wave of missions advance. If revival is the spark that ignites the spreading of the good news in human hearts, then prayer is certainly the wind that fans the flames into a spiritual forest fire!

Prayer is vital to missions. If the fourth wave of modern missions is to be the greatest thrust of all, then global united prayer will be an essential aspect.

We now turn to the power of unity as the third factor in missional success.

Unity—The Fruit of Humility and Prayer

When our hearts are revived by an encounter with Jesus, we can pray in humility for God's will to be done. Humble prayer brings our hearts into unity with God and each another.

One of the remarkable characteristics of the Triune Godhead is the power of unity that emanates from God's Oneness. There is something otherworldly about loving unity—especially when compared to human sin and divisiveness. People who humbly work together as one can accomplish much more than those who operate alone.

The Bible teaches, "Two people are better off than one, for they can help each other succeed. . . . A person standing alone can be attacked and defeated, but two can stand back-to-back and conquer. Three are even better, for a triple-braided cord is not easily broken" (Eccles. 4:9–12).

There is great power in unity, and this power is not simply the addition of numbers. It is the exponential multiplication of effect that comes through working together. When people are unified, God promises that "you will chase your enemies, and they shall fall by the sword before you. Five of you shall chase a hundred, and a hundred of you shall put ten thousand to flight; your enemies shall fall by the sword before you" (Lev. 26:7–8 NKJV).

Unity does not just add strength, it greatly multiplies it. A united leadership or nation has an authority and strength that is very difficult to stand against. And this is not simply a human phenomenon. Psalm 133 teaches that when people dwell together in unity, that is where "the Lord [has] commanded the blessing" (v. 3 NKJV).

A primary pathway to unity is humility—confessing our sins, submitting to one another, and considering others more important than ourselves (Phil. 2:1–11). When human beings humble themselves, accept others' ideas, and lovingly strive to work for the common good, amazing things can happen.

Robert Greenleaf spent over thirty years as an executive with AT&T, one of the world's largest corporations. As he analyzed the strength of that company, and that of other organizations in which he was called upon to lead, he came to a conclusion that the best type of leadership was team leadership, where unity in decision making and diversity of gifts was critical for success. He saw that high-level unity not only increases productivity, but greatly protects the corporation and all of its workers.[11]

If it's true in business, it's even more important in the church.

The longest prayer of Christ recorded in the New Testament is found in John 17. In part, Jesus interceded, "I am praying not only for these disciples but also for all who will ever believe in me through their message. I pray that they will all be one, just as you and I are one—as you are in me, Father, and I am in you. And may they be in us so that the world will believe you sent me" (John 17:20–21).

The greatest conduit of authenticity that is available to the body of Christ is the demonstration of loving unity and oneness of mind. That's something Satan can't counterfeit. In a world of selfishness and broken relationships, unity is attractive, a novelty, and an example to follow. Jesus said that if his disciples were one, as he and the Father are one, then the entire world would be affected by the gospel. According to Jesus' prayer, a completely unified church is crucial to the completion of world evangelism. Our lack of unity is our greatest shame and is open admittance of failure to follow the teachings of Christ.

God uses revival to humble and purify human hearts. As believers pray for his purposes to be done in their lives, communities, and nations, the dynamic of unity is released to bring multitudes to Christ. In every missionary wave we will consider, unity among believers was a key catalyst for success. Loving unity multiplies results.

It was a privilege for me to work with Rev. John Gimenez of the Rock Church in Virginia Beach, Virginia, on the 1980 and 1988 Washington For Jesus rallies. "Brother John" was the man that God used to bring about the largest unified gathering of the church in the history of the United States at the time—involving hundreds of thousands of people.

He is a most unlikely hero. John was a Puerto Rican immigrant who was raised in Spanish Harlem in New York City. At an early age he became a drug addict and spent time in and out of prison. Then Jesus Christ got hold of his life, and with his evangelist wife, Anne, John founded a thriving church on the East Coast. It was to this man, who had a deep heart for unity in the body of Christ, that God gave the vision to bring the American church together for repentance and prayer. Because of his commitment to unity, he was one the heroes of the American church in the latter part of the twentieth century.

If the words of Jesus in John 17 mean anything, then people who do the most to promote Christian unity in a city, state, or nation will make the greatest contribution to world evangelization. Unity among believers is vital to missional advance.

We will see many amazing examples of unity in the different waves of missions.

God's Providence

Another premise in analyzing the various waves of Christian evangelism over the past two thousand years is that God is the sovereign director of history. From the beginning, he has had a plan for redeeming the world—a fact the Bible shows on nearly every page from the beginning of creation in Genesis 1 to the new heavens and earth described in Revelation 21.

God's wise sovereignty begins with his choice of missionaries in each era. We will see that he commissioned first the Jews, then Gentiles

throughout the Roman Empire, next monks, and in later centuries Protestant Europeans and Americans. In the twenty-first century, I believe the
leading edge of missions will be populated by Africans, Latinos, Islanders,
and Asians. We will also see his providence in the role of women, children, and youth in missions. God has a divine plan for individuals, races,
and cultures in the cause of world evangelism.

Theologians may disagree on how God's sovereignty interacts with
human free will, but no one denies that God is sovereign and that his
providence is a major force in the development of history—including
nations. American pastor A. W. Foljambe presented this idea in a message
to his congregation on January 5, 1876, when he said, "The more thoroughly a nation deals with its history, the more decidedly will it recognize and own an over-ruling Providence therein, and the more religious a
nation it will become; while the more superficially it deals with its history,
seeing only secondary causes and human agencies, the more irreligious it
will be."[12]

In the 1850s Arnold Guyot, the first geology instructor at Princeton
College, believed that God had purposes for whole continents, not just
nations. He taught his Princeton students that Asia was the continent of
origins (the human family, its races, civilizations, and religions), Europe
was the continent of development (arts and learning), and America was
the continent of propagation (Christian missions to the world).

Guyot stated:

In the grand drama of man's life and development, Asia, Europe, and
America play distinct parts, for which each seems to have been admi-
rably prepared. Truly no blind force gave our Earth the forms so well
adapted to perform these functions. The conclusion is irresistible—
that the entire globe is a grand organism, every feature of which is the
out-growth of a definite plan of the all-wise Creator for the education
of the human family, and the manifestation of his glory."[13]

Another interesting aspect in God's grand plan for world missions
over the past two thousand years was his choice to guide Christian missions in a *westward direction*.

If you look specifically at God's leading in Paul's missionary journeys, you will see God's plan for the gospel to proceed westward from Israel. Paul's trips are preeminent in Acts, as they are representative of God's mission vision.

Paul's first mission trip was an exploratory one. On his second missionary journey (Acts 16:6–9), Paul and his team stayed in Galatia because the Holy Spirit had kept them from going into the Roman province of Asia (both provinces are in modern-day Turkey). As they traveled toward Mysia, they tried to go north into Bithynia, but again they were stopped by the Holy Spirit. Instead they were led all the way to the westernmost point of the continent of Asia—to Troas.

It was here that Paul received the vision of a Macedonian man (Acts 16:9–10) imploring them to cross the sea to Macedonia (in present-day Greece). The Holy Spirit was revealing to Paul and his team that God's wise plan of the reaching the world must continue in a westward direction. Apparently God had prepared the geographical area we call Europe for the next major expansion of Christian civilization.

On Paul's third missionary journey, he seemed to understand God's intentions to expand the gospel to the west. On his fourth mission trip, while a prisoner, his missionary outreach took the message of Christ all the way west to Italy (Rome). Paul's eyes were set beyond there as far as Spain (Rom. 15:24). The Iberian Peninsula is the westernmost point of mainland Europe.

Following the decline and collapse of the Roman Empire (between the second and fifth centuries), Christian missions and civilization took root on European soil as if it had been prepared for this assignment. Then, following the Renaissance and Reformation, God "lifted a curtain" on the New World, extending Western civilization and missions outreach to what would become the Americas. Catholic missionaries labored in South and Central America, and Protestant missionaries, Pilgrims, and Puritans evangelized in the north.

The United States of America would be born in 1776 largely because of the First Great Awakening and the spiritual and political revolution that would establish it as the leading nation in Christian missions from the latter part of the nineteenth century until today.[14]

God's next step in the westward movement of Christian missions would be to the islands of the Pacific in the nineteenth century and then on to southern Africa and Asia in the twentieth. The final section of the globe still awaiting sizeable momentum in missional activity is the Hindu–Buddhist–Muslim sections of southern, central, and western Asia and northern Africa. When Christian missions explodes in the twenty-first century in this highly populated area dubbed "the 10/40 Window," the good news will have circled the globe and made its way back to Jerusalem (more on the Back to Jerusalem movement in chapters 7 and 8).

Technology

Finally, we will note that the advance of Christian missions is greatly aided or abetted by the development of civilization and technology throughout history. During the time of the early church, Roman civilization had created both political and practical bridges for the dissemination of the gospel. However, prior to the advent of ocean-going vessels, advanced navigational techniques, and printing presses, missions outreach was limited.

The emergence of modern science in Europe—based on the Christian worldview—and the inventions of the compass in Portugal (twelfth century) and the printing press in Germany (1450) opened whole new horizons of discovery, human development, and missionary outreach.[15] The next stage was the Industrial Revolution, which helped create the modern middle class and capital markets, which in turn created opportunities for both prosperity and evangelization worldwide. More recently, the invention of the airplane, telephone, radio, television, medical vaccines, and Internet have opened vast new horizons for communicating the good news of Jesus to every person on earth.

All of these advances were not made at random. There is a divine mind and hand behind the progress of history. God has used the developments of civilization and technological invention in positive ways to advance his kingdom purposes on earth. We will discuss the factor of technology in each of the modern waves of missions.

We now return to the eighteenth century, where a post-Reformation world had created a religious battleground in Europe, and where the cause of world evangelization had been placed on the back burner.

But God has prepared a count and a cobbler for such a time as this. These two will lead us into the modern era of missions.

Part 2

The Modern Era of Missions

"To know the will of God, we need an open Bible and an open map."

—William Carey

"If a commission by an earthly king is considered a honor, how can a commission by a Heavenly King be considered a sacrifice?"

—David Livingstone

"The Bible is not the basis of missions; missions is the basis of the Bible."

—Ralph Winter

Chapter 5

The First Wave of Modern Missions: To the Coastlands (1730s to 1850s)

THE REFORMATION of the sixteenth century—led by Martin Luther, Ulrich Zwingli, and later John Calvin—brought great resurgence of personal faith and biblical teaching in Roman Catholic Europe. But to its leaders, theology was primary and missions secondary. In fact, Martin Luther was certain of Christ's imminent return and claimed that the Great Commission was binding only upon the New Testament apostles.[1]

Oh well, we all make mistakes.

Still, in response to the Protestant Reformation, a renewal in Catholic missions surged during this time period under the leadership of Ignatius Loyola and the Society of Jesus (the Jesuits) and Francis Xavier, a Jesuit pioneer who brought the gospel to Japan between 1542 and 1552 and who died while en route to China. During the fifteenth and sixteenth centuries, other Catholic monks joined the ranks of Spanish and Portuguese explorers in taking their faith to the New World.[2] It would not be until the 1700s that the modern Protestant missions movement would be born through a German nobleman—Count Nikolaus von Zinzendorf— and his unassuming group of religious refugees.

Zinzendorf and the Moravians

Count Nikolaus Ludwig von Zinzendorf was born in 1700 into wealth and nobility. According to Ruth Tucker, author of the very popular missions history *From Jerusalem to Irian Jaya:*

> Count Zinzendorf was one of the most influential mission leaders of the modern Protestant missionary movement. He pioneered ecumenical evangelism, founded the Moravian church, and authored scores of hymns; but above all else he launched a world-wide missionary movement that set the stage for William Carey and the "Great Century" of missions that would follow.[3]

In 1716 Zinzendorf, in conjunction with four teenage friends, started The Order of the Grain of Mustard Seed, a club that was committed to advancing the good news. In 1719 the youthful Zinzendorf visited an art gallery in Denmark, where he viewed a painting—Domenico Feti's *Ecce Homo*—that showed Christ with a crown of thorns with this inscription: "All this I did for you. What are you doing for me?" This vision of Christ's sacrifice and our responsibility to tell others changed Zinzendorf's life and became the "mustard seed" of modern missions.

Zinzendorf's call to ministry crystallized in 1722, when Protestant refugees, fleeing persecution from the European religious wars, sought refuge on his estate in Berthelsdorf, Upper Lusatia (present-day Saxony), later named Herrnhut (which means "under the watch, or protection, of the Lord"). On August 13, 1727, revival broke out in a Lutheran church service, which had a profound impact on the community. Two years later an around-the-clock prayer watch was started (beginning with twenty-four people and eventually building up to seventy-two) that went on for over one hundred years. By 1738 the first Moravian missionaries had arrived in the Caribbean, some of them by the only means possible— by selling themselves into slavery. As tearful families bade farewell to the young missionaries as they boarded ships headed for the New World, the courageous Moravians pioneers told them that Jesus was worthy to receive the due reward of his sufferings.[4] Most would never return.

In subsequent decades Moravian missionaries would share Christ's message throughout Scandinavia, the New World, and beyond. Zinzendorf spent thirty-three years of his life overseeing a network of growing Moravian missionaries that eventually numbered in the hundreds.[5] The Moravians are one of the few groups since the time of the early church who demonstrated a missions commitment to reach the world for Christ.

William Carey

As important as the example of the Moravians was to this renewed thrust to evangelize the world, it would take the heroic labors of an English cobbler to fully launch the modern age of world missions. Ruth Tucker agrees with the historical consensus that "the beginning of the Protestant missionary movement is conveniently dated as 1800. William Carey is the grand patriarch, and the setting is the subcontinent of India where the world's oldest and most complex religions were born."[6]

I will use Tucker's excellent portrait of William Carey to paint a brief picture of this missional pioneer.

For three hundred years Christian explorers had been sailing the far reaches of the world. As early as 1600, Queen Elizabeth I had granted a charter to the East India Company, which would put the British (and Christian) stamp on India for centuries to come.[7]

William Carey was born in 1761 near Northampton, England. At an early age he was apprenticed to a shoemaker and later married his master's sister-in-law, Dorothy, in 1781. Carey had an unusual burden for the unreached (heathen), and while sharing his burden one day with a group of ministers, one of them exclaimed: "Young man, sit down. When God pleases to convert the heathen, He will do it without your aid or mine."[8]

Carey didn't agree with that theological assessment, and in 1792 he published *An Enquiry Into the Obligation of Christians to Use Means for the Conversion of the Heathens* (shortened title). In his eighty-seven-page treatise he applauded the Moravians for their missions zeal.[9] After tracing the history of Christian missions, Carey used twenty-one pages of the book to list the countries of the world and their populations, lamenting that out of a then-global population of 731 million, "420 million lie in pagan darkness."[10] He called on the Christians of his day to use every means possible to reach them, and ended his appeal with these stirring words: "What a heaven it will be to see the myriads of poor heathens who have been brought to the knowledge of God. Surely a crown of rejoicing like this is worth aspiring to. Surely it is worthwhile to lay ourselves out with all our might, in promoting the cause, and the kingdom of Christ."[11]

Soon thereafter, he started the Baptist Missionary Society, based on Isaiah 54:2–3, while uttering the words most associated with him: "Expect great things from God; attempt great things for God." Carey set sail for India with his young family on a Danish vessel on June 13, 1793, and arrived in Calcutta on November 19. This uneventful five-month trip by ship to a distant unreached coastland of the world would set the stage for what Kenneth Scott Latourette would term "The Great Century" of missions activity.[12]

Carey's young family eventually moved two hundred miles north of Calcutta to Malda. These were hard years of battling foreign diseases, learning the local languages and dialects, and trying to understand the complexities of a teeming Indian culture. Carey's wife, Dorothy, experienced bouts of depression and mental instability, which even led to her following her husband around the crowded marketplaces and crazily shouting that he was being unfaithful.[13] Despite these and many other difficulties, First Baptist Church was started in India in 1795 with four members—all Englishmen! After seven years of toil among the Bengali people, Carey could not claim even one Indian convert.

In 1800 the Carey family moved back nearer Calcutta, to Serampore. Dorothy died here at the age of 51 in 1807. William Carey then focused the remaining thirty-four years of his life on pioneering missionary efforts, which began to bear fruit. Thirteen of those years were spent in marriage to Lady Charlotte Rumohr. Joshua Marshman and William Ward would join him for twenty-five of those years, forming one of the most famous missionary teams in history.

One of Carey's greatest gifts to the Indian people was his translation work of the Bible into many Indian languages and dialects. By 1824 he had overseen six full translations of the Bible and twenty-four partial translations. By the end of his life, the number would grow to forty-six translations—though he lost many of his precious manuscripts in a warehouse fire in 1812.

Carey did extensive medical work in northeast India and also started Serampore College in 1819. Tucker summarizes Carey's great missionary efforts with these words:

> By 1818, after twenty-five years of Baptist missions to India, there were some six hundred baptized converts and a few thousand more who attended classes and services. Carey died in 1834, leaving a legacy for other missionaries to follow. In addition to evangelism, education, and translation, he had focused his attention on social issues—particularly in his long struggle against widow burning and infanticide. . . . Carey was ahead of his time in missionary methodology. He had respect for the Indian culture and never tried to import Western substitutes. His goal was to build an indigenous church "by means of native preachers" and by providing Scriptures in the native tongue. To that end he dedicated his life.[14]

Bruce Shelley comments on Carey's impact on world missions: "William Carey introduced Christians to missions on a grander scale. He thought in terms of the evangelization of whole countries. . . . Above all, he saw that Christianity must be firmly rooted in the culture and traditions of the land in which it is planted. For all these reasons and more Carey gained the title 'Father of Modern Missions.'"[15]

While William Carey is rightly credited with launching the modern wave of world missions, and Baptist missions in particular, he was not the first Baptist missionary to sail the seas. That distinction falls to liberated slave George Lisle, who was the first black ordained minister in America and America's first Baptist missionary. In 1782, ten years before Carey's trip to India, Lisle, his wife Hannah, and their four children landed in Kingston, Jamaica. He began itinerant preaching in 1784, started the first church in Jamaica, and saw hundreds of converts to Christ before his death in 1826.[16]

Many other missionaries also began to travel by ship to the various seaports of Africa, Asia, the New World, and the Pacific. They included

Adoniram Judson, the American-based Protestant missionary who landed in Burma (also known as Myanmar today) in 1812, and Robert Morrison, missionary to China who was the first to translate the Scriptures into Chinese. The good news of Christ was finally leaving the confines of Europe and European-settled colonies in a new wave of Protestant missionaries committed to reaching the populated, trade-oriented coastal cities of the world.[17]

The missional keys of the first wave of modern missions were similar to those of the early church.

Revival!

Herrnhut, Wesley, Whitefield, and the First Great Awakening

The Moravian community had been transformed by spiritual revival during the summer of 1727, and the power of this awakening to repentance, love, forgiveness, and holy living became the fountain of their missionary endeavors. In 1729 a yet-unregenerate John Wesley encountered the revival faith of the Moravians on a ship making its way to the American colony of Georgia. Upon returning to England, he sought out Peter Boehler, a Moravian pastor who encouraged him to "preach faith until he had faith." Soon thereafter, John Wesley's heart was "strangely warmed," and the Methodist Revival, a part of the First Great Awakening, began to impact all of England.[18]

John Wesley visited the Moravian community of Herrnhut in 1738 and said that it was like "heaven on earth." By the time of his death in 1791, there were one hundred thousand Methodists in Britain and the New World, and many of them were joining the growing missions movement.[19]

An American-grown version of the First Great Awakening was another major driver in the surge of Christian missions during the early part of the eighteenth century. Most historians associate its birth with Congregational minister and theologian Jonathan Edwards. His sermon series on saving faith in the fall of 1734 led to an awakening in Northampton, Massachusetts, resulting in twelve hundred conversions.[20] For ten years the awakening spread through the American colonies with an esti-mated fifty thousand—or one out of every five—colonists making deci-sions for Christ. It was during that period that spiritual foundations were laid for the American Revolution.[21] At the same time, George White-field, an original member of John Wesley's Oxford Holy Club, preached throughout England and the Colonies, sometimes speaking to crowds as large as thirty thousand on Boston Common. George Whitefield was the most recognized preacher in colonial America. The revival he led pro-vided a foundation for Christian missions for decades to come.

Prayer

The Watch of the Lord and Under a Haystack

The Moravian prayer watch at Herrnhut was the seedbed for Mora-vian outreach. The equation was simple: when people pray fervently for the world, God often allows them to be answers to their own prayers. Thus, two years after the Moravians began their round-the-clock praying, the first Moravian missionaries began to go out.

The First Great Awakening was also built on fervent, united prayer. Jonathan Edwards wrote a famous treatise on "concerts of prayer" in 1747, instructing believers on both sides of the Atlantic to unite in prayer for world evangelism. In direct opposition to the European religious wars, these concerts of prayer united Christians from many denominations around the need to ask the Lord to send laborers into his harvest.[22]

In 1806 a group of students at Williams College in Massachusetts were caught in a rain storm and retired to a haystack to wait it out. Samuel J. Mills shared his burden while under the mountain of straw, and fervent prayers were offered for the evangelization of the world. The impromptu prayer meeting concluded with this affirmation of the Great Commis-sion: "We can if we will!" Soon a student-led prayer movement spread to other college campuses and was an integral part of the Second Great Awakening, the Evangelical Revival of the early nineteenth century. The first American missionary to Asia, Adoniram Judson, was called to the mission field by reading an account of the Haystack Prayer Meeting.[23]

Unity

Among Different Cultures and Denominations

The Moravian Revival began in a Lutheran church service on August 13, 1727, when religious refugees of different nations and cultures repented of their sins, reconciled broken relationships, and committed to live in loving unity with each other. Their "love feasts," a shared meal around a time of communion, echoed early church commitment and fellowship and became well known throughout the world. During the First Great Awakening in America, pastors in various towns would preach the gospel together in the streets—demonstrating the union that Christ's love can bring. These were small steps during a very polarizing time. But the increase of unity among God's people was a fulfillment of the prayer of Jesus in John 17 and allowed the Holy Spirit to awaken and send his workers to new fields of the world.

The combination of revival, increased prayer, and demonstrated love among these eighteenth-century believers was a key to their vision for missions outreach. The Moravians set the early example, and now many thousands were following. But there were other important factors in the rise of this first wave of modern missions to the coastlands of the world.

Providence

Protestant Europeans

God chose the Jewish people to be the first members and missionaries of the early church and its mission. As Gentiles were converted to faith in Christ, they joined the growing mission force. For the next fifteen centuries, as far as records exist,[24] the vast majority of Christian missionaries witnessed within the Roman Empire (before and after its fall in 476). These early missionaries, like the apostle Paul, were guided by God to take the Christian message westward from Jerusalem to the outer reaches of the empire. Notable exceptions were the apostle Thomas, who, according to legend, was the first to take the gospel to India,[25] and Saint Patrick, a Roman citizen from what is now Britain, who shared his faith in Christ cross-culturally with the people of Ireland, where he had once been a slave.[26] During the Middle Ages, monastic orders, such as the Irish monks, the Dominicans, the Franciscans, and later the Jesuits, continued to expand the outreach of the gospel. The monastic communities were both centers of learning and beacons of missionary advance during this chaotic era.[27]

The first wave of modern missions saw the rise of the Protestant European and American missionary taking Christ's good news beyond the confines of Europe to coastal ports in the Americas, the islands of the Pacific, and (to a lesser extent) the major port cities of Asia and Africa. As the first push of early church mission was westward, so the modern rebirth of missions also went primarily in the same direction. The Americas were the first stop by both Catholic and Protestant missionaries, with the ports of the South Pacific and Asia as the next westward destinations. We will return to this theme of the westward expansion of the gospel in later chapters.

The evidence of history indicates that God had a wise global plan for evangelizing the world that shouts out during this particular era, "Go west, young Protestants, go west!"

Technology

Johann Gutenberg and the Age of Exploration

A major impetus to Christian outreach during this period was Gutenberg's invention of the printing press by 1450, which led to the first mass printing (180 copies) of the Bible in 1455. During the first modern wave of missions, Bibles and Christian books, tracts, and periodicals were instrumental in disseminating the good news of Jesus Christ into coastal cities. At the turn of the twenty-first century, *Time* magazine named Johann Gutenberg the most important person of the past five hundred years because the printing press vastly accelerated the multiplication of knowledge throughout the world.[28]

Roman roads and the Greek language were essential to the spread of the gospel in the first centuries. In the age of exploration, the invention of the compass and other advanced navigational techniques allowed seafaring ships to become technological tools that aided the first wave of modern missions. Most of the colonial-era explorers were God-fearing men with a sense of adventure. David Howard, author of *Jesus Christ: Lord of the Universe, Hope of the World,* believes that one of the main motives for the explorations of Marco Polo and Christopher Columbus was evangelization.[29] Though there is evidence that the Chinese had discovered America two generations before Columbus and other Spanish, English, and Portuguese explorers,[30] it was Christian-based Western explorers including Columbus, Vasco Da Gama, Magellan, and James Cook who provided the transportation necessary for evangelistic outreach. Since ships went to bustling port cities, this first wave of modern missions followed the coastal routes. God was using the infrastructure of the day to advance his global purposes.

This era also saw the expansion of the "bivocational missionary" who often used business or government appointments to advance the gospel. The Moravians were famous for their work ethic and business enterprises. Others followed their example. David Howard comments:

> William Carey, the father of the modern missionary movement, supported himself and others in his mission by running an indigo factory as well as being a salaried professor of Sanskrit at the University of Calcutta.... Because Henry Martyn was not allowed to go to India as a missionary, he went out as a chaplain for the East India Company. Robert Morrison, who translated the Bible into Chinese, also supported himself by being an interpreter for a trading company. Many do not realize that David Livingstone became a consul for the British government in Africa and pictures often show him wearing the hat of his office.[31]

Because of the passion of a count—Nikolaus von Zinzendorf—and the vision and perseverance of a cobbler—William Carey—the modern age of missions was born in the eighteenth century. Year by year, more and more missionaries boarded the ocean-going vessels of the age to take the claims of Christ into the seaports of the world.

Millions of people lived in these coastal regions where trade and commerce were booming. Others lived inland—in Asia, Africa, and other parts of the world.

Next enters a man whose travel logs eventually made him the most intriguing celebrity of the nineteenth century. He was a renowned adventurer and explorer who gave thirty years of his life pulling back the veil on an entire continent of unknown tribes and people. But in his heart, he was a missionary.

Chapter 6

The Second Wave of Modern Missions: To the Interiors (1850s to 1930s)

THE SECOND WAVE of modern missions—"The Great Century"—began with David Livingstone's groundbreaking exploration of the African interior, and with other missionaries such as Hudson Taylor sharing the gospel in the inner regions of China. Missional advance was greatly expanding at this time, starting in the seaports of the world and then moving *inland*. This was the next logical step in bringing the gospel of Jesus Christ to every person on earth. No one symbolized this era of rugged missionary penetration more than the adventurer and explorer David Livingstone— one of the nineteenth century's most interesting personalities.

David Livingstone

David Livingstone, "the apostle of Africa," was born in Blantyre, Scotland, on March 19, 1813. Strongly devoted to Christ, he applied to the London Missionary Society in 1838 to serve in China but was turned down because the opium wars had closed the country. He later met Robert Moffat, a pioneer missionary in southern Africa, who inspired him to join his efforts on the Dark Continent.[1] He was ordained as a missionary in 1840 and set sail for South Africa, arriving in early 1841. He worked among the Bakwain people for a number of years; married Mary Moffat, the eldest daughter of Robert Moffat; and was responsible for the conversion of Sechele, the chief of the tribe. Sechele would be used by God to preach the gospel to his own people for many years.[2]

J. H. Worcester quotes Livingstone during this early period: "The work of God goes on here notwithstanding all our infirmities. Souls are gathered in continually and sometimes from among those you would have never expected to see turning to the Lord. Twenty-four were added to the church last month, and there are several inquirers."[3]

In 1852 Livingstone sent his family back to England and began the first of three major expeditions to explore and evangelize the African interior. The watchword of his life had become "Fear God and work hard."[4] In 1855 he crossed the entire continent—never before accomplished by a European—and received a gold medal from the London Geographical Society. Livingstone then returned to his family in England and wrote his notable *Missionary Travels* in 1857. This book inspired hundreds of eager missionaries to go to the African continent in the coming decades.

Livingstone made a triumphant return to Africa in 1858 with his wife and eldest son on the "Ma Robert" steamer to explore the Zambezi River. The trip ended in disappointment when it was found that the Zambezi was not fully navigable, and Livingstone's family returned to England. Livingstone persevered in exploring and sharing Christ in Central Africa, leading to his authoring another popular book, *The Zambesi and Its Tributaries*, which was critical of the Muslim slave trade in the region. He remarked: "Cannot the love of Christ carry the missionary where the slave trade carries the trader?"[5]

Further travels—Livingstone attempted to locate the headwaters of the Nile River and ended up discovering Lake Tanganyika in 1867—led to his final book, *Last Journals*. Livingstone suffered many illnesses and scrapes with death during his final expeditions. On November 10, 1871, he shared the now-famous rendezvous with Henry M. Stanley, who had been sent by the *New York Herald* to find him in the depths of Africa. Stanley was a self-professed atheist who later converted to Christ because of Livingstone's example.

Two years later, in 1873, sick and pushing onward, David Livingstone was found dead in a hut—praying on his knees for Africa. His physical heart was fittingly buried in African soil, but his body was eventually brought back to England, one of Britain's most beloved sons being laid to rest in Westminster Abbey. Upon hearing of the death of the legendary explorer, Florence Nightingale wrote to her sorrowing friend in a letter, "God has taken away the greatest man of his generation, for Dr. Livingstone stood alone."[6]

Worcester explains, "As a missionary explorer, he stood alone, travelling 29,000 miles in Africa, adding to the known portion of the globe about a million square miles. . . . He was the first European to traverse the entire length of Lake Tanganyika. . . . He greatly increased the knowledge of the geography, fauna and flora of the interior, yet never lost sight of the great objects of his life, the putting down of the slave trade, and the evangelization of Africa."[7]

Livingstone had exposed the breadth and beauty of the African continent for others to evangelize and disciple. As a missionary, he was a forerunner, a trailblazer opening the country for Christianity to enter in.

J. Hudson Taylor

On the opposite side of the world, fearless missionaries were advancing the faith into the inner regions of "darkest Asia." Their greatest challenge was China. Carl Lawrence and David Wang explain in *The Coming Influence of China:* "The early missionaries established beachheads for the gospel along the coast. Hudson Taylor spearheaded the movement into the inland. Today, their work is exploding with growth."[8]

James Hudson Taylor was the man God chose to penetrate the mysterious interior of "the Middle Kingdom." Fred Barlow explains, "'He must move men through God by prayer,'—that was the philosophy of J. Hudson Taylor, first missionary to the interior of China and the founder of the China Inland Mission. And from that December day when as a teenager he heard from heaven, 'Go for Me to China,' this young Englishman set out to prove his philosophy. That he did so successfully and miraculously makes for some of the most exciting reading in the records of evangelism."[9]

Hudson Taylor was born in 1832 in Barnsley, Yorkshire, England. His father was a chemist and Methodist lay preacher. Taylor worked as a teenager in Drainside, Hull, to gain medical experience, and then sailed for China in 1853 at the age of twenty-two. He served other workers and learned the Chinese culture in Shanghai during this time. But Taylor was never happy living with other missionaries. Less than a year after he arrived in China he began making journeys into the interior. On one of those trips, he traveled up the Yangtze River and stopped at nearly sixty settlements never before visited by a Protestant missionary.[10] Thus began over fifty years of ministry in China that would see Taylor launch and organize the largest missions thrust into the nation and greatly change the face of Protestant missions.

Early in his travels, Taylor concluded that to reach the Chinese people he needed to become one of them. J. C. Pollock tells us that Taylor changed his dress and dyed his hair to look more Chinese—which wasn't easy for a Caucasian Brit. He later exclaimed: "You would never know me were you to meet me in the street and the other Chinese. . . . I am not suspected of being a foreigner."[11] Taylor did ten missionary journeys in his first two years (1854–56). He and his family returned to England in 1861 to write about the mission to China, recruit more missionaries, and raise funds for the work.

On June 25, 1865, in England, Taylor dedicated himself to God for the founding of a new society to undertake the evangelization of the "unreached" inland provinces of China. He founded the China Inland Mission together with William Thomas Berger shortly thereafter. In less than one year, they accepted twenty-four missionaries and raised over £2,000 (about $200,000 today). In early 1866, Taylor published the first edition of the *Occasional Paper of the China Inland Mission*, which later became *China's Millions*. Taylor was establishing the first Protestant faith mission, a model others would follow in subsequent years.

Hudson Taylor summarized his new mission this way:

The China Inland Mission was formed under a deep sense of China's pressing need, and with an earnest desire, constrained by the love of CHRIST and the hope of His coming, to obey His command to preach the Gospel to every creature. Its aim is, by the help of GOD, to bring the Chinese to a saving knowledge of the love of GOD in CHRIST, by means of itinerant and localized work throughout the whole of the interior of China.... The Mission is Evangelical, and embraces members of all the leading denominations of Christians.[12]

Taylor determined to use the following methods in his outreach to the Chinese people:

1. That duly qualified candidates for missionary labor should be accepted without restriction as to denomination, provided there was soundness in the faith in all fundamental truths.

2. That all who went out as Missionaries should go in dependence upon GOD for temporal supplies, with the clear understanding that the Mission did not guarantee any income whatever; and knowing that, as the Mission would not go into debt, it could only minister to those connected with it as the funds sent in from time to time might allow.[13]

In addition:

The Mission is supported entirely by the free-will offerings of the LORD's people. The needs of the work are laid before GOD in prayer, no personal solicitations or collections being authorized. No more is expended than is thus received, going into debt being considered inconsistent with the principle of entire dependence upon GOD.[14]

Taylor and his enlarged family of twenty-four new missionaries returned to China in 1866, put on their Chinese clothes and hairstyles, and set about with renewed zeal to win the inland masses. Their team traveled down the Grand Canal of China to make their first settlement in Hangzhou. In 1868 the Taylors took a party of missionaries up to Yangzhou to start a new work. Despite various accidents, regular bouts with disease, and the rigors of missionary life, many Chinese came to the Lord.

Pollock writes:

> In that eventful year of 1870, Hudson Taylor was still a young man
> in his thirties. The China Inland Mission included thirty-three mem-
> bers and occupied stations in three of China's twelve provinces. After
> sixteen years of demanding, health-breaking missionary service at
> great personal cost (the loss of his wife and three of his beloved chil-
> dren out of seven), Hudson hadn't lost sight of the goal. In fact, he felt
> more certain than ever that God had called, and was still calling him
> to evangelize the whole country of China—as impossibly huge as the
> task seemed.[15]

Over the remainder of his life, Hudson Taylor would expand the outreach of the China Inland Mission to eight hundred missionaries serving in 205 mission stations that led 125,000 Chinese to Christ.[16] Hudson
Taylor died in 1905—leaving behind one of the greatest outreach legacies
in the annals of Christian missions.

The dynamic China Inland Mission continued to prosper. By the
1930s the missions membership had grown to 1,285. Total income since
1900 had reached $20 million unsolicited; there were between three and
four thousand Chinese workers with the mission; and the baptisms in
the first three decades of the 1900s had totaled more than one hundred
thousand.[17]

Hudson Taylor's influence on the Protestant missions movement was
immense. Few missionaries in the twenty centuries since the apostle Paul
have had a wider vision and have carried out a more systematic plan of
evangelizing a broad geographical area than did James Hudson Taylor.
He had a knack for organization, and he possessed a magnetic personality
that drew men and women to him and his point of view. The China Inland
Mission was his creation and was a model for future faith missions.

Ralph Winter and Steve Hawthorne comment: "God strangely honored him because his gaze was fixed on the world's least reached peoples.
Hudson Taylor had a divine wind behind him. . . . It was his organization, the China Inland Mission—the most cooperative servant organization yet to appear—that eventually served over 6,000 missionaries,

predominantly in the interior of China. It took 20 years for other missions to begin to join Taylor in his special emphasis—the unreached, inland frontiers."[18]

C. T. Studd, John Mott, and the Student Volunteer Movement

During this second wave of modern missions, another vital movement of the Holy Spirit was increasing the ranks of missionaries worldwide—especially the inland frontiers. The Student Volunteer Movement (SVM) was born at a Mount Hermon Missions Conference in Massachusetts in 1886. Its beginning had occurred even earlier when some students at Cambridge University in England—the Cambridge Seven—turned their backs on various career ambitions and committed their lives to foreign missions.

The group included cricketer C. T. Studd, who went to China in 1885 and served there for fifteen years, followed by six years in India. Studd then spent the remainder of his life in central Africa where he started the Heart of Africa Mission, which later became the Worldwide Evangelization Crusade (now WEC International). One of my first missions instructors in New Zealand was Ivor Davies, a WEC missionary who had been part of the Congo Revival of the 1930s, following in C. T. Studd's footsteps.

The Student Volunteer Movement prospered for some fifty years, during which time it was instrumental in sending 20,500 students to the foreign missionary field, most of them from North America. It is estimated that during the early twentieth century student volunteers constituted half of the total Protestant overseas missionary force.[19]

The greatest mobilizer of these student missionaries was John R. Mott, who attended a small university in Iowa. In the summer of 1886, Mott represented Cornell University's YMCA at the first international, interdenominational student Christian conference ever held. At that conference, which gathered 251 men from eighty-nine colleges and universities, one hundred men—including Mott—pledged to work in foreign missions. Two years later, the Student Volunteer Movement for Foreign Missions was born.

Mott was extremely successful as a missions mobilizer. He wrote sixteen books, crossed the Atlantic over one hundred times and the Pacific fourteen times (averaging thirty-four days on the ocean per year for fifty years), delivered thousands of speeches, and chaired innumerable conferences.[20] Many others joined him in calling the youth of their generation to global missions.

Ruth Tucker states:

John R. Mott, perhaps more than any other individual, influenced the surge of students into overseas missions. . . . The highlight of Mott's career as a missionary statesman was the Edinburgh Missionary Conference of 1910, which he organized and chaired. This ten-day conference, composed of 1,355 delegates, was the first missionary conference of its kind . . . a high point of missionary enthusiasm; and the call to evangelize the world "in this generation" was still in the air.[21]

The "Great Century" would spill over beyond 1914 and on through the second and third decades of the twentieth century, with many notable missionaries joining the swelling tide of world evangelism. Let's now look at the keys to missional success that accompanied this remarkable era.

Revival!

The Second Great Awakening

What paved the way for the second wave of modern missions was a related spiritual awakening known as the Second Great Awakening, also called the Evangelical Revival, which impacted the British Isles, other European nations, and especially the United States during the 1790s to 1830s. Revival historian J. Edwin Orr writes:

There is no doubt that the general awakening of the 1790s and 1800s, with its antecedents, was the prime factor in the extraordinary burst of missionary enthusiasm and social service, first in Britain, then in Europe and North America. . . . William Carey, a founder and pioneer of the Baptist Missionary Society, was one of a group who first set up in England the simultaneous prayer union that spread throughout evangelical Christendom and achieved its avowed purpose in the revival of religion and the extension of the Kingdom of Christ overseas. . . . The revival proved dynamic.[22]

The Evangelical Revival especially touched college campuses on both sides of the Atlantic, and in the United States was a leading impetus for the student missions movements that would emerge later in the century. In the United States, this renewal produced evangelists who greatly influenced the northeast and southern regions of the country.

Another outpouring in the United States, known as the Great Revival, began in 1857 in response to an October stock market crash and the ensuring panic that followed. During these years revivalist Charles Finney, who had come to Christ during the Second Great Awakening, preached in Rochester, New York, where over one hundred thousand people made commitments to Christ, with lasting spiritual fruit in that city for over one hundred years.[23]

Prayer

Jeremiah Lanphier and Fulton Street

Revival can be conceived of not only as a fire but also as a gun, delivering the bullets of the Holy Spirit's work into the lives of many. If revival is the gun of Christian missions, then certainly prayer is the gunpowder that delivers the ammunition.[24] The Haystack Prayer Meeting, concerts of prayer, and the growing Evangelical Revival prayer movements had a great impact on the missionary success of the Great Century.

One of the most unusual prayer movements of the period was the lay-led "noon prayer meetings" that helped ignite the Great Revival of 1857. The man credited with this prayer revival was Jeremiah Lanphier, a New York merchant. On September 23, 1857, Lanphier climbed creaking stairs to the third story of an old church building on Fulton Street in Lower Manhattan and sat down to wait. He had placed a sign on the street below that read "Prayer Meeting from 12 to 1 o'clock—Stop 5, 10, or 20 minutes, or the whole hour as your time admits." For the first few days, only a couple of people joined him. A week later, six people trudged in. On October 14, 1857, the nation was staggered by the worst financial panic in its history. Banks closed, men were out of work, and families went hungry.

The following week twenty had gathered to pray, and the next week—forty.

In a few short weeks following the crash, the Fulton Street Prayer Meeting had taken over the whole building, with crowds of more than three thousand. Within six months, ten thousand businessmen were gathering daily in New York City for prayer.

The revival of prayer soon jumped the Atlantic Ocean and also spread across the United States, impacting most of the major cities in the nation. After a number of years, and continuing during the American Civil War, it is estimated that more than one million people came to Christ, including 43,388 Southern Methodists, 135,517 Northern Methodists, and 92,243 Baptists.[25] This particular prayer movement was primarily led by laymen, not clergy, and formed the backdrop of the large missionary surge that went around the world in the coming decades.

Unity

Mount Hermon (1886) and Edinburgh (1910)

The revivals and their corresponding prayer thrusts created a strong bond between believers, breaking down denominational barriers and encouraging people to work together in the spirit of Jesus' prayer in John 17:21–22. In this passage Jesus shows the direct correlation between unity and world evangelism.

The 1880s to 1930s also saw the emergence of some of the world's first united missions conferences focused on completing the Great Commission. Evangelist D. L. Moody had called for the Mount Hermon Conference in 1886, the first united national intercollegiate Bible convention in America. The immediate outcome of the Mount Hermon Conference was that one hundred young men decided to give their lives to missions— among them the young John R. Mott, who would lead the charge of the

Student Volunteer Movement for decades. As previously mentioned, Mott later served as organizer of the Edinburgh Missionary Conference of 1910—the first missionary conference of its kind that united the church around the world to complete the task of world evangelization.[26]

Church historian Kenneth Scott Latourette believes 1815–1914 was an extremely important period in the history of mankind and Christian advance. The ranks of missionaries grew exponentially during this period. Latourette notes that in 1914 the staff of Protestant missionary organizations was said to number 5,462. Even as late as 1895, about two-thirds were from the British Isles, approximately one-third were from the United States, and between 2 and 3 percent were from the continent of Europe. By 1914 about half were from the United States, two-fifths from the British Isles, and nearly one-tenth from the continent of Europe.[27]

Providence

Women Join Global Missions

During this second great wave in modern missions, God directed his people to reach out beyond the coastal areas of the world to the peoples in the interiors of previously unknown and unexplored nations. It was risky to venture to these inland unknowns due to the prevalence of diseases, fierce or unfriendly tribes, language barriers, and strange customs and manners. But starting with David Livingstone in Africa, and being inspired further by Hudson Taylor's brave accomplishments in China, thousands of young missionaries ventured forth to answer the call.

A remarkable change in missions during this era was the involvement of women. Women had always served as vital disseminators of the gospel through childbearing, family responsibilities, and one-on-one impartation of faith. During the Middle Ages, many Christian women in Europe were forced to marry their Viking conquerors and leave their homelands as domestic slaves. One positive consequence of this barbarity was the introduction of faith in Jesus into what is now Sweden, Norway, Denmark, and Finland. During the medieval period, various nuns, including the famed Bridgett of Kildare and Claire of the *Poor Claires* (a group related to St. Francis of Assisi), were vital in the spread of Christian faith.

But the nineteenth century brought a freedom and release to women in missions that greatly impacted the history of world evangelism. By 2001 nearly 60 percent of the world's missionaries were women. That trend began during the second wave of modern missions—and was catapulted into being through the American Civil War, when six hundred thousand men lost their lives. With such a significant loss of male leadership, earning ability, and traditional roles in some families, women stepped up to rebuild both the American nation and also the American church.

David M. Howard gives this perspective:

> The Civil War strongly affected the progress of women in missions. It was an educative force in America, for through it women were driven to organize because of their patriotism and their pity for the fighting men. In the ten years following the War, scores of organizations, including many new missionary societies, were launched. . . . The first single woman on record who was sent to a foreign land was Betsy Stockton, and she was black.[28]

This new opportunity for single women joining the growing missionary army produced such missionary heroes as Lottie Moon in China, the "patron saint" of Southern Baptist Missions (1873–1912); Irish missionary Amy Carmichael, who served in India for fifty-five years (1895–1951); and British pioneer Gladys Aylward, who also served in China (1932–1957).

Technology

The Industrial Revolution

One of the major drivers of the second wave of modern missions was the Industrial Revolution, which created stronger and more affluent middle classes in both Europe and the Americas. There was more money to make, more raw materials that needed to be procured, and greater wealth being produced that could be used to fund world evangelization.

The Industrial Revolution from the eighteenth to the nineteenth century was a period of great change. Developments in agriculture, manufacturing, mining, and transportation produced vast social and economic changes around the world. This significant turning point in history catapulted many nations—and missions—into the modern world we know today.[29]

Starting in the later part of the eighteenth century, a transition began toward machine-based manufacturing in parts of Great Britain's economy, which until that time had been based solely on manual labor and draft animals. First came the use of machines to power the textile industries, increased productivity in producing metals, and the widespread use of coal. Increased mechanization enabled bigger and better canals to be built in a much shorter time period, followed by vastly improved roadways and, by the 1830s, railways. The invention of the steam engine was a great boon to increased industrial production. The development of metal machine tools in the first two decades of the nineteenth century caused exponential growth in economic capacity. These powerful innovations spread throughout Europe and North America during the nineteenth century, creating a great deal of wealth and a growing middle class.

Christian missionaries greatly benefited from the Industrial Revolution, which provided faster travel on coal-fired steamships and supplied better medicines to combat disease. The revolution also produced a higher standard of living that increased giving to mission causes, and a general optimism that included the American vision of Manifest Destiny—a term originally used in 1845 to describe American expansion across the continent to the Pacific but later expanded to include America's "mission" in the world.[30]

As Great Britain earned the title of global missions leader of the nineteenth century, the ground was being prepared for American ascendancy to that position in the twentieth century. Ruth Tucker states:

> By the middle of the twentieth century the United States had become the missionary "sender" of the world. . . . They were different in many ways from their missionary forebears. They were women in increasing numbers, and they were better educated with stronger theological views—university educated student volunteers. . . . Like their predecessors, they were hardy individualists, tempered by waves of revivals

and spurred on by a pioneering spirit—and the latest technology—
to advance the Gospel.[31]

Latourette's "Great Century" (1815–1914) proved a great boon to
world evangelization. But the best was yet to come.

Chapter 7

The Third Wave of Modern Missions: To Unreached Peoples (1930s to Present)

THE FOCUS OF MISSIONS in the twentieth century progressed from the coastlands and interiors to a more defined target: *unreached peoples* numbering thirteen thousand worldwide. These are the nations, or ethnic groups, mentioned in the New Testament (*ethnos* or *ethne* in Greek). This was to become the Third Wave—the biggest wave yet. With most of the seaports and major inland areas seeing increased missionary activity, it was a natural step to focus like a laser beam on those who had been over-looked. This required an increasingly diverse array of approaches to sharing the good news.

Here was God's twentieth century bull's-eye: *reaching the unreached peoples by using specialized outreach methods.*

Ruth Tucker explains:

The typical nineteenth-century missionary, if there was one, was an evangelist. His time was largely consumed with saving souls and planting churches. Even if he practiced medicine or translated Scripture, he was first and foremost a preacher of the gospel. By the twentieth century that concept of a missionary was changing. Missionary work was becoming far more diversified. By mid-century many mission societies had been founded for the express purpose of promoting certain mission specialties, and in the decades that followed, it was assumed that a missionary would specialize in a particular aspect of ministry.[1]

This "honed and skilled" approach would lead to the greatest harvest century of all time. In fact, more people would give their lives to Christ worldwide during the twentieth century than the previous nineteen centuries combined.[2] If Latourette was right in labeling the nineteenth century "the Great Century" of Christian expansion, then the twentieth century will certainly go down in history as "the Greater Century" of Christian missions.[3]

I will initially highlight three missional pioneers who serve as forerunners and innovators during this period: Donald McGavran, Cameron Townsend, and Ralph Winter. McGavran was one of the first to teach the concept of "people groups." Townsend applied that understanding to language translation and founded one of the world's largest missionary organizations, Wycliffe Bible Translators. Winter mainstreamed the focus on unreached people groups for the global church. Together, these three helped set the aims and strategy of the twentieth-century wave toward completing the Great Commission.

Donald McGavran

Donald McGavran (1897–1990) was a missionary, educator, author, and founding dean of Fuller Theological Seminary's School of World Mission in Pasadena, California. He was born December 15, 1897, in India, the son and grandson of missionaries. At the age of thirteen, his father took Donald to Scotland, where he was serving as one of the 1,355 delegates to John R. Mott's famed Edinburgh Missionary Conference. After they returned to the United States, Donald grew up and later served in the army during and after World War I. In 1919, during a YMCA Conference in Lake Geneva, Wisconsin, McGavran dedicated his life to going where God sent him and carrying out his will.[4]

He married Mary Howard in 1922, and in 1923 the young couple were commissioned as missionaries by the United Christian Missionary Society. They sailed back to India, where they served for the better part of three decades in educational and evangelistic ministry. McGavran was in charge of the missions school system in Harda for eight years, and then, after a sabbatical during which he completed a PhD at Columbia University, they returned to India. At that point he served in Jubbulpore and later in Takhatpur, where he managed a leprosarium and was involved in evangelism among various castes.

After thirty-one years on the foreign field, the McGavran family returned to the United States on furlough. Although it was Donald and Mary's intention to return to India, the mission sent him to other parts of the world to do research into the growth of churches planted by the mission as well as other related Christian groups. He also was a guest lecturer at several seminaries in the United States, Puerto Rico, Jamaica, the Philippines, Thailand, and Zaire (Congo) in the period 1954–1960. He began to teach and write extensively about the theories he had developed during his time in India, and which he wrote about in his groundbreaking book *The Bridges of God* (originally titled *How Peoples Become Christian*) published in 1955.

Starting in 1961, with the birth of the Institute for Church Growth, and later as founding dean of the Fuller School of World Mission (1965–71), a program he was closely affiliated with until his death in 1990, McGavran taught a missiological perspective that was to have an enormous influence not only on the way Protestant evangelicals practiced missions but on their understanding of church life generally.

From his years of service, McGavran developed a methodology of *contextualization* of the gospel for each culture that was crucial for its widespread advance among an exploding world population. Commenting on McGavran's *The Bridges of God*, Ralph Winter says it contained

the classic summons for missionaries to utilize the "bridges" of family and kinship ties within each people group thereby promoting "people movements" to Christ. . . . To Christianize a whole people, the first thing not to do is snatch individuals out of it into a different society. Thus a Christ-ward movement within a people can be defeated either by extracting the new Christian from their society (i.e. by allowing them to be squeezed out by their non-Christian relatives) or by the non-Christians so dominating the Christians that their new life in Christ is not apparent. . . . It is important to note that the group decision is not the sum of the separate individual decisions. The leader makes sure that his followers will follow. The followers make sure that they are not ahead of each other. Husbands sound out wives. . . . As the group considers becoming Christian, tension mounts and excitement rises. Indeed, a prolonged informal vote-taking is under way. A change of religion involves community change. Only as its members move together does change become healthy and constructive.[5]

McGavran's concepts of contextualization "people movements" and the idea that cultures were to be "redeemed" by "redemptive analogies" made a significant contribution to church-planting and evangelism movements in the twentieth century. McGavran helped the missions surge move from the seaports and interiors into sociological groups within each nation while urging missionaries and their converts to think through the most effective means of planting fast-growing churches and indigenous missions movements.

Cameron Townsend

Cameron Townsend was another twentieth-century missions pioneer who helped the church realize its need for specialized tasks to complete the Great Commission. According to Ralph Winter, William Cameron Townsend was one of the three most influential missionary leaders of the last two centuries.[6] His specialty was languages, and out of his vision came the world's foremost linguistic organization, Wycliffe Bible Translators, which is committed to translating the Bible into every language on earth. Townsend believed that "the greatest missionary is the Bible in the mother tongue. It needs no furlough and is never considered a foreigner."[7]

Cam Townsend (as he was commonly known) was born in California in 1896 during a time of economic recession. He was raised in the Presbyterian Church and decided to stay in California, enrolling in Occidental

College in Los Angeles. During Townsend's collegiate junior year, John R. Mott visited Occidental and challenged students to give their lives to the evangelization of the world in this generation. Townsend met with Mott and joined the Student Volunteer Movement (SVM), committing his life to the Great Commission. He had joined the National Guard in 1917 and was prepared to serve his country in a time of war. But when he met a missionary on furlough who challenged him to obey his SVM commitment and go to the mission field instead of the battlefield, Townsend responded. He applied for and received a discharge in order to go on a one-year missions trip to Guatemala. He arrived in August of 1917.

An early incident on this trip had a profound impact on his life, changing his personal perspective and the course of missions history. Townsend was living among the Cakchiquel Indians, and one day a man came to him and looked curiously at his Spanish Bible. Townsend explained that it was the Word of God, who was the Creator of all mankind. The man replied bluntly, "If your God is so smart, why doesn't he speak my language?" Townsend was stunned to realize that this man and the other two hundred thousand Cakchiquel people living in Guatemala had no access to Scripture because they knew little or no Spanish.

The sobering remark left Townsend with a burden for the thousands of individuals, and hundreds of other tribes, without one page of Scripture in their language. For the next thirteen years Townsend dedicated himself to the Cakchiquel Indians, during which time he translated the Bible into their language. This feat took ten years.

Concerned about other minority tribes, Townsend returned to the United States and opened Camp Wycliffe (named after John Wycliffe, who had been the first to translate the Bible into English) in Arkansas in the summer of 1934. The camp was designed to train young people in basic linguistics and translation methods. Two students enrolled. The following year, there were five in attendance. From this small beginning came the ministry of the Summer Institute of Linguistics and, in 1942, the establishment of Wycliffe Bible Translators—currently one of the largest Christian missionary organizations in the world.

Townsend cared deeply about language translation and serving people's practical needs, which led him to work as a goodwill ambassador to many nations. He worked in Guatemala from 1917 to 1934 and in Mexico from 1935 to 1946, where he became good friends with President Lazaro Cardenas, about whom he wrote a biography in 1952. He lived in Peru from 1946 to 1963, and after 1968 he made eleven trips to the former USSR from his home in North Carolina. At the time of his death in 1982, he was a personal friend to forty-two heads of state around the world and supervised thousands of translators working hard to put the Bible into the more than 6,900 languages on earth. Today Wycliffe translators serve in over ninety nations and are zeroing in through "Vision 2025," an extraordinary effort to put the Scriptures into the remaining 2,200 languages that have yet to be translated.[8]

Cameron Townsend, affectionately called "Uncle Cam" by his associates, had found a "specialty area" of ministry that could greatly speed the sharing of the good news—putting God's Word into the mother tongue of every person on earth. In Claude Hickman's biography of Townsend, he states:

> Uncle Cam was credited with beginning the final missions era that we are living in today. It is an era that focuses not on just reaching continents and inland countries, but on every distinct ethnic group, or people group in the world. This people group focus, taken from the original meaning of the word 'nations' (ethnos) as it was used in the New Testament and in the Great Commission, is the commitment to pioneer into every ethno-linguistic group.[9]

Ralph Winter

A third modern missionary pioneer—Dr. Ralph Winter (1924–2009), founder of the U.S. Center for World Mission—would take the concepts of Donald McGavran and the methods of Cameron Townsend and crystallize them to form the next crucial step of missions outreach. This third wave of modern missions, which focused on *hidden* or *unreached peoples,* would become the passion of Winter. It was Winter who coined the term "hidden peoples" at his speech to the 1974 Lausanne Congress, the latest gathering in a series of conventions dedicated to completing the Great

Commission. His phrase referred to people groups that were hidden from *our* sight—not that were hiding from us.

It was during this presentation that Winter shifted global mission strategy from a focus on political boundaries to a focus on distinct people groups. Winter argued that instead of targeting countries, mission agencies needed to target the thousands of people groups worldwide, over half of which had not been reached with the gospel message. Billy Graham, the convener of the 1974 Congress, remarked: "Ralph Winter has not only helped promote evangelism among many mission boards around the world, but by his research, training and publishing he has accelerated world evangelization."[10]

For the past forty years, reaching the unreached peoples of the world has been the most prominent battle cry of the Third Wave.

Ralph Winter was born on December 8, 1924, in Los Angeles, California. During his studies at Cal Tech, he joined the U.S. Navy. They sent him back to finish his bachelor of science degree because they needed engineers. He finished in two and a half years. After joining the training program for Navy pilots, the war ended and he went on to earn his MA at Columbia University and PhD at Cornell University. He then decided to finish the seminary studies he had started at Fuller Theological Seminary by getting a BD at Princeton Theological Seminary.

In 1951 Winter married Roberta Helm, and five years later their young family went to serve as Presbyterian missionaries to Guatemala from 1956 to 1966. It was in Guatemala that Winter, with others, developed and spearheaded the Theological Education by Extension (TEE) program—the precursor for modern-day theological distance education programs and the multi-campus models used by schools and seminaries today. The TEE idea inspired a movement, and soon similar programs were replicated around the world.

After delivering what became a defining message at the 1974 Lausanne Congress, Winter and his wife, Roberta, felt the Lord leading them to a place where they could tackle cultural and linguistic barriers hindering the sharing of the gospel with all peoples. In November 1976, they founded the U.S. Center for World Mission on a thirty-five-acre college campus in Pasadena, California, with no staff, one secretary, and $100 in cash. Their faith story is told by Roberta in her book *I Will Do A New Thing* (originally titled *Once More Around Jericho*). Throughout his life, Winter founded a number of organizations and journals, including the William Carey Library (1969), the William Carey International University (1977), *Mission Frontiers* magazine (1979), and the International Society for Frontier Missiology (1986).[11]

Winter summarized the challenge facing twentieth-century missions forces and how that challenge led to the notion of targeting unreached peoples:

> Landing at an airport, whole square blocks and buildings suddenly come into focus. Details not visible before become clear as a bell. This is what happened when Protestants finally decided to send their own missionaries out across a strange and mysterious world. The Biblical command was simple: "disciple the nations."
>
> But as soon as the missionaries "landed" they discovered that *winning individuals* was unexpectedly difficult. Most "people" lived within the tight grip of a "people," a social structure, a culture, an extended family. Missionaries found that individuals could not very easily be pried out so as to "be saved" one by one. . . . Sooner or later, missionaries learned that the highest quality church movements were those that did not try to tear up or replace the social fabric of the "nation" to which they were sent.
>
> Thus arose the concept of "peoples" (within which people live). Donald A McGavran, a third-generation missionary in India, championed a somewhat novel idea: that missionaries ought not to consider their job done, nor assume that they have given any individual a real chance to accept Christ *unless that person can become part of what he called a "people movement."* [emphasis Winter's]
>
> This radical idea required missionaries to do more than evangelism. They had to plant churches. A further logical conclusion is then that unless "a people movement to Christ" is set in motion, the basic missionary accomplishment has not yet been made. This means it is not good enough for there to be a few Christians, some

missionaries, even a Bible translation, if there is not yet a substantial, indigenous social movement within which new believers can belong. This now precisely defines what is or isn't an "unreached people." A people group can be reached only if somehow there is achieved "a viable, indigenous, evangelizing church movement that is a people movement."[12]

Thus twentieth-century missiologists began to organize the remaining task of Christian missions by unreached peoples. Donald McGavran had discovered the need, Cameron Townsend had organized a specialty ministry to confront it, and Ralph Winter had coined the term and explained the concept that would drive the third wave in modern missions. Millions of individuals, thousands of churches, and hundreds of organizations would rise to meet that need in the coming years.

The Century of Specialization

The third wave of modern missions swelled significantly throughout the twentieth century. Two world wars didn't stop its forward momentum, and technological marvels certainly aided its growth. As modern inventions led to the increased specialization of labor and production, God seemed to nudge this latest group of missional pioneers to greatly diversify their approach in sharing the gospel with people. Peoples were different, cultures were unique, times were changing.

This diversification paralleled the economic diversification spawned by the Industrial and Information Revolutions. A significant element in the shift in the missionary paradigm from individual efforts to *networks of collaboration* was the emergence of a variety of specialized organizations in the entrepreneurial style of Western society that began to be applied to evangelism, discipling, and church planting.

The breadth of this specialization in ministry over the past one hundred years is difficult to represent. I will list just a sampling of the incredible diversity the Holy Spirit added to world evangelization during the rising tide of the Third Wave:

- Crusade evangelism as typified by Billy Graham, Luis Palau, and Greg Laurie.
- Campus ministry through organizations such as Campus Crusade for Christ, the world's largest single missionary organization, with over twenty-five thousand missionaries.
- Young people in missions as typified by Operation Mobilization, Teen Missions, and Youth With A Mission.
- Healing campaigns with powerful figures like Oral Roberts, T. L. Osborn, and Reinhard Bonnke.
- Outreach to global political leaders pioneered by Abraham Vereide in the 1930s and continuing with Doug Coe and the Fellowship Foundation.
- Ministry to business people such as the Full Gospel Businessmen's Fellowship.
- Women's outreach through groups like Women's Aglow.
- Christian television and radio, such as the Christian Broadcasting Network, the Trinity Broadcasting Network, and GOD TV. The Far East Broadcasting Company and Trans World Radio continue to be key players in restricted nations.
- Internet websites and chat rooms that transcend closed national borders.
- Athletic outreach through the Fellowship of Christian Athletes (FCA).
- Use of ships in ministry through Operation Mobilization and Mercy Ships.
- Christian humanitarian aid through nongovernmental organizations (NGOs) like World Vision International.
- Church planting movements (CPMs) that cause multiplication of indigenous churches that in turn plant other churches, sweeping through a population segment. Most of these movements are led by lay leaders.

The explosion of Christian specialty ministries in the past hundred years is truly breathtaking and unique in history. This rich diversity of emphasis and methods has allowed billions of people to come in contact with the good news of Jesus Christ. As multitudes have come to Christ for salvation, the tide of missionary recruits has broadened to include people of all colors.

This is one of the quietest revolutions of our lifetime. It will be a crowning hallmark of the coming Fourth Wave.

Majority World Missionaries

Here's what happened with very few taking notice: *The second half of the twentieth century saw the strength of the global church move into the Southern Hemisphere* as Majority World missionaries began to take their place in the annals of Christian missions as the up-and-coming missions force.

Luis Bush, who in 1989 coined the term "10/40 Window,"[13] and who served as the leader of the AD2000 movement, describes the phenomenon of Majority (or Two-Thirds) World evangelism this way: "Missionaries from the Two Thirds World? Just a few years ago the idea would have seemed unthinkable. But not now! Today the rapidly growing Two Thirds World mission force is one of the most remarkable factors in world evangelism. . . . This vital resource has the potential to reach the whole world with the Gospel. The consequences could be incalculable."[14]

Though there were numerous Majority World missionaries in the third wave of modern missions in the twentieth century, I will briefly mention five people—two Koreans, one Indian, one Chinese, and one Nigerian—that symbolize the changing face of missions.

David Yonggi Cho

David Yonggi Cho was a young Assemblies of God pastor who made his way to the capital city of Seoul, Korea, in 1956. He began a small church that grew to about fifty believers the first year. Depending on all-night prayer and retreating to various "prayer mountain" sites to cry out to God for revival and world evangelization, Cho's church grew to 400 members by 1959.

Focusing on prayer, faith healing, and cell group ministry, the Yoido Full Gospel Church expanded in 1982 to accommodate ten thousand people per service (with nearly 250,000 members), then reached 400,000 in 1984, 700,000 in 1992, and 850,000 in 2010.[15] In the 1990s Cho decided that rather than expanding further, the church should establish satellite churches in other parts of the city and around the world. Since the year 2000, Yoido has sent out over one thousand missionaries and planted new churches in a number of nations.

Today Yoido Full Gospel Church in Seoul, Korea, is the world's largest Christian congregation. One hundred and fifty years ago there were no Christian churches in Korea and, of course, no Korean missionaries.

Samuel Kang

Samuel Kang and his wife, Sarah, left South Korea for Nigeria in 1980, when there were only ninety-three Korean missionaries worldwide. During the next eleven years, Samuel and Sarah raised a family, planted Nigerian churches, and started a Bible college for Nigerian pastors. Kang returned to Korea in 1991 and currently leads an ambitious twenty-five-year plan to help South Korea send out more missionaries than any other country. He launched a mission agency and became an academic dean at Chongshin University and director of the Korea World Mission Association (KWMA). Kang and the association plan to send one hundred thousand full-time Korean missionaries by 2030. They hope to mobilize 50 percent of Korean churches to be involved in missions, recruit one of every three hundred Korean Christians to become missionaries, adopt two hundred unreached people groups every five years, and send one million tent-making missionaries (bivocational workers) into difficult-access countries by 2020.[16]

Robert Moll details the amazing growth in Korean missions, pointing out that South Korea sends out more missionaries than any other country except the United States; in 1991 they sent out 1,200 missionaries, up from eight missionaries just eleven years before! Today that number has reached 13,000.[17]

K. P. Yohannan

K. P. Yohannan grew up in a small village in South India. After eight years of missions service in the subcontinent, he went to the United States for his theological studies and also pastored a church. However, he was unable to forget the untold millions who have not heard about the love of Christ in the 10/40 Window.[18] In 1979 he resigned from his pastorate to focus on missions. From that small beginning, today *Gospel for Asia* has become an effective mission movement with thousands of workers—most of them Indians—in eleven Asian nations. K. P. Yohannan spends a significant part of his time traveling to many nations and speaking on behalf of the suffering and needy in our world. His call to the body of Christ is to become the Lord's authentic followers and impact their generation for Christ. He has authored more than two hundred books published in Asia and seven in the West. As a new breed of Indian missionary evangelist, Yohannan believes that,

> Around the world today, the Holy Spirit is breaking over Asian and African nations, raising up a new army of missionaries. Thousands of dedicated men and women are bringing the salvation story to their own people—millions of souls in closed countries who would probably never learn about the love of God by any other means. These humble, obscure pioneers of the gospel are taking up the banner of the cross where colonial-era missions left off. They are the next wave of mission history—the native missionary movement.[19]

Yohannan's focus is on his native India—the second most populous nation on earth. Another native movement is underway in China, the world's second most populated country.

Liu Zhenying (Brother Yun)

Liu Zhenying, known to much of the world as "Brother Yun," is an example of the growing impact and outreach of the Chinese church. Though closed off to the rest of the world for most of the past six hundred years, China now reports one of the largest and fastest-growing church movements on record. It is led largely by a courageous group of persecuted pastors and underground house church leaders.

Brother Yun became a Christian at the age of sixteen when his father was miraculously healed of cancer.[20] After asking God to provide him a Bible, Yun fell to his knees, committing to "devour its contents like a hungry child" and share it throughout his region of China. Under constant threat of arrest, he began to travel to villages and towns in southern China, sharing the good news and seeing thousands come to Christ. Brother Yun was eventually caught and arrested (three times) and spent many years in harsh Chinese labor camps and prisons. During one stint in prison in 1984, he miraculously fasted without food or water for seventy-four days, his weight dropping to sixty-six pounds. God's miraculous healing of Yun led to many conversions.[21] During this same time period, many courageous house church leaders were being hunted and imprisoned, including Brother Zhen and Brother Xu. They were a part of a vast network of house church leaders who saw millions of people turn to Christ during the revival decades of the eighties and nineties.

Brother Yun now travels the world as an advocate for Chinese house churches and the Chinese revival. One of his favorite subjects is the Back to Jerusalem movement, a commitment by the Chinese church to take the gospel across Central Asia to the city where it all began. The vision was started in 1921 in Shandong province by a Christian named Jing Dianying, who encouraged believers to commit to five things they could personally do to complete the Great Commission: sacrifice, abandonment, poverty, suffering, and even death.[22] By the 1940s there were twenty thousand Chinese believers enlisted in this effort throughout China. Today the commitment stands at over one hundred thousand committed to going. Brother Yun says that the Chinese church is willing to pay the price.[23]

Adelaja Sunday

Adelaja Sunday, a native of Nigeria, is an African example of the growing Two-Thirds World mission force. Sunday was invited to study in the USSR before glasnost (openness), at the age of nineteen. He came to faith only weeks before traveling to the USSR. In 1993 Sunday went out as a bivocational missionary to Kiev, Ukraine, where the Lord then spoke to him about starting a church. Today Sunday is pastor of the Embassy of the Blessed Kingdom of all Nations, also known as the Embassy of God, which after ten years of existence, has grown to more than 23,000 members. Over seventy other churches have been planted by the Embassy of God in Ukraine and other nations, including Russia, Belarus, Moldova, Georgia, the United States, India, and the United Arab Emirates. The mother congregation in Kiev is Europe's largest church—led by this enterprising African.[24]

Let that sink in. One hundred and fifty years ago, Africa was the Dark Continent of witchcraft, slavery, and few believers. It was exclusively a mission field. European missionaries went to evangelize Africa.

Today an African is the pastor of Europe's largest church.

Each of Adelaja Sunday's "twelve disciples" takes responsibility for between 1,000 and 2,500 members, all of which meet in cell groups. Sunday rents a sports arena and holds several services each weekend. He aims to send his twelve closest associates out to plant sister churches throughout the world. Adelaja Sunday is a new breed of Africa pastor/missionary/evangelist who is taking missions from Africa back to the continent from which it came and also to many other nations.

These five stories are typical of the new breed of mission pioneers that are becoming the current and future face of missions.

Incredible Harvest

The twentieth century saw an amazing tidal wave of global missions expansion in the Two-Thirds World developing nations, especially those located in the Southern Hemisphere:

- The continent of Africa was 4 percent Christian in 1900. In 2000, 50 percent of those south of the Sahara Desert professed faith in Christ—over 300 million people.[25]
- In Latin America there were 50,000 Protestants (people who claimed to be born again) in 1900. In 2000 there were 100 million, of whom most were Pentecostals.[26]
- Korea boasts seven of the eleven largest churches in the world, is 30 percent Christian, and is the second largest sending nation in the world with 13,000 missionaries serving in other lands.[27]
- China went from one million believers in Christ in 1900 to an estimated forty to one hundred million in 2000.[28] David Aikman,

former *Time* bureau chief in Beijing, believes that number could be as high as 150 million.[29]

Luis Bush rightly comments: "The spread of Christianity into the non-Western world is one of the great success stories of all history. . . . This massive extension has been a working faith. No other cause in history has fostered such far-reaching humanitarian efforts of goodwill as has Christianity."[30]

The Century of Acceleration

We were born into an amazing time in missions history. The Third Wave has cascaded across the continents of the world bringing hundreds of millions of people into the blessings of the gospel. Much of that growth is due to the Pentecostal Revival which began in 1906 and brought a "power dimension" to missions outreach by adding 640 million people to the ranks of the church. Grant Wacker credits the Pentecostal movement with launching over three hundred Pentecostal denominations and their missions enterprises from the United States alone.[31]

Luis Lugo, director of the Pew Forum, describes the impact of the Pentecostal Revival and its advance of missions in Latin America:

It's a combination of immigration in which a lot of Latinos are already Pentecostal and the conversion taking place in the Catholic Church among those converting to Pentecostalism. . . . It's really evangelism on steroids. This may well be the most dynamic religious movement in the world today in terms of growth and breadth.[32]

Yet the greatest building wave of missions is the hundreds of primarily Pentecostal Latin American, Asian, and African church planters that are starting churches and focusing their prayers and efforts on unreached peoples. The mission field is becoming the missions force. Scott Moreau of Wheaton College says:

The day of Western missionary dominance is over, not because Western missionaries have died off, but because the rest of the world has caught the vision and is engaged and energized. Today's missionary is as likely to be a black African in Europe as a northern Indian in south India or a Korean in China. In addition, mission leaders are placing a new focus on Asia, where 60 percent of the global population lives. The same is true of Africa and the Middle East.[33]

The third wave of modern missions has birthed an amazing array of ministry specialties and people of many nationalities that are reaching people for Christ. As a result, as the twenty-first century dawned, 3,500 churches were being started every day, and 70,000 people were being saved worldwide each day—including 28,000 in China and 20,000 in Africa.[34]

How did that happen? We now turn to the key factors that made up the Third Wave. They share a common trait: the gospel of Jesus Christ truly going global.

Chapter 8

Going Global

JUST AS WAVES in a rising tide build upon one another and reach farther and farther onto the beach, the waves of Christian missions across the centuries built on the success of the previous ones to extend the kingdom of God.

Here's the historical recap. After Jesus' death and resurrection,

- the early church proclaimed his good news throughout the *Roman world* and beyond;
- monks and monasteries expanded the reach of the church in Europe and parts of Asia during the Middles Ages;
- the Moravian Brethren and William Carey helped to launch the first wave of modern missions to the *coastlands* of the entire world during the age of seafaring exploration;
- David Livingstone and Hudson Taylor led a courageous generation of Second Wave missionaries beyond the accessible seaports into the *interiors* of Africa and Asia during the great advance of the nineteenth century;

- Christian faith in the twentieth century became the world's first *global* faith by targeting the remaining *unreached peoples* of an exploding world population but "shrinking" planet (due to technological advances); and
- the Third Wave saw great specialization in ministry and the emergence of *Majority World missionaries* taking their place in the growing global missions enterprise.

After centuries of building momentum, missions outreach has finally gone global. Let's examine the key factors that contributed to its worldwide surge.

Factor One—Revival!

God's Presence and Power All Over the World

As we've noted, spiritual awakenings always precede missionary advance. The original Pentecost outpouring was the dynamite of early church outreach. Seventeen centuries later, the Moravian renewal rekindled the spark of taking Christ's message to those who hadn't heard. The Great Awakenings of the eighteenth and nineteenth centuries propelled the advance to the coastlands and provided the motivation to reach the interiors of many unevangelized countries.

The missionary results of the Third Wave were far greater than the previous two waves, in part because the twentieth century saw greater revivals than any other era. It saw another unusual feature: *revival on a global scale.*

One awakening that seemed to launch this great century of outreach was the Welsh Revival that began in 1904 under the leadership of Evan Roberts.[1] Roberts was studying at Bible college when God challenged him to take a strong message about sin back to his youth group in Wales. The message was: (1) confess all past sin, (2) repent and make restitution, (3) surrender to the Holy Spirit in obedience, and (4) publicly confess Christ.[2] A revival broke out that spread across Wales, leading even hardened coal miners to Christ and closing down some of the prisons because of a subsequent lack of crime. The Welsh Revival was characterized by great joy and singing—and often no preaching—as people came under the influence of the Holy Spirit.[3] News of the revival spread to many nations around the world and led to an outpouring of God's Spirit in Pyongyang.

Historian J. Edwin Orr states the significance of the Welsh Revival:

The farthest felt happening of the decade was the Welsh Revival, which began as a local revival in early 1904, moved the whole of Wales by the end of the year, and raised up Evan Roberts . . . while filling simultaneously every church in the nation. The Welsh Revival was the farthest reaching of the Awakening, for it affected the whole of the evangelical cause in India, Korea and China, renewed the revivals in Japan and South Africa, and sent a wave of awakening over Africa, Latin America, and the South Seas.[4]

In 1906 African America William J. Seymour started revival meetings on Azusa Street in Los Angeles that included healings, speaking in tongues, and the baptism of the Holy Spirit. People came from all over the world to visit this "Pentecostal Outpouring," which eventually birthed such vital denominations as the Assemblies of God, the Church of God, and the Church of God in Christ. According to historian Vinson Synan, Pentecostal missions today are the fastest growing part of world evangelization. Synan comments: "The Azusa Street revival is commonly regarded as the beginning of the modern Pentecostal movement. . . . In addition to the ministers who received their Pentecostal experience directly at Azusa Street, thousands of others were influenced indirectly."[5]

China also saw a spiritual awakening in 1906 under the leadership of missionary Jonathan Goforth, who had read a tract in 1905 by American revivalist Charles Finney. Entitled "Break Up Your Fallow Ground," the tract brought Goforth under conviction of sin, which led to his sharing at missions stations throughout China. Everywhere he went, the Spirit fell.[6] This revitalization and expansion of the Chinese church laid the foundation for the greatest numerical revival of the twentieth century—the explosion of the Chinese church under communism from 1949 to the present. As already stated, between forty to one hundred million Chinese have given their lives to Christ during the past sixty years—thus becoming the greatest awakening in history of a single nation. China's revival began in the rural areas, but is now spreading to the cities and intelligentsia of the nation.

A spiritual awakening broke out in Africa during the 1930s, which became known as the Congo Revival. The ripple effect soon spread to other nations on the continent. It was a move of God accompanied by signs and wonders, including a manifestation of the Holy Spirit called "fixations," in which a person's arm would supernaturally be "fixed" in the air until someone repented of sin. Prior to repentance, the arm couldn't be budged until the desired person repented. Many healings also took place during this season of the outpouring of God's Spirit on African soil.[7]

The Korean nation saw a jolt of the Holy Spirit from 1907 to 1910, which especially impacted the north.[8] Following the Korean War and the dividing of north and south, the revival traveled to Seoul, where a great surge of conversions and church growth has taken place from the 1950s to today. Nearly one-third of South Korea's citizens are now born-again Christians, and the Korean Revival has been the fuel behind South Korea becoming the world's second largest sending nation.

In 1949 God used Scottish preacher Duncan Campbell to spark a revival in the Hebrides Islands off the coast of Scotland. Campbell was directed to the islands by the Holy Spirit, who introduced him to two women who'd been praying for years and were told of his coming in advance. When Campbell began to preach, some church buildings shook, and people came under conviction of sin while walking up the pathway to the churches. The Hebrides Revival, like the Welsh Revival, was characterized by great joy with many young people singing on the beaches of the islands at all hours of the night and day.[9]

In the 1960s and 1970s the Jesus Movement and charismatic renewal sprang up around the world with many hippies and young people coming to Christ during the days of the Western youth revolution. Though not a full-blown revival, the charismatic renewal was an important time of revitalization for numerous people and denominations, as individuals became filled with the Holy Spirit and empowered to share their faith.[10]

Another outpouring of God's Spirit took place in Indonesia in the 1960s through evangelists such as Mel Tari, who saw many people healed and some even rise from the dead.[11] Because of the power of the revival, Indonesia, the world largest Muslim nation, could lose that distinction because nearly 20 percent of Indonesians now call themselves Christians. The growth of the church continues in Indonesia.

In summary, the twentieth century saw revival movements spring up around the world. It is out of those revivals—especially the building force of the Pentecostal and charismatic renewals—that the third wave of modern missions found its fuel for advancing the cause of world evangelization.

Factor Two—Prayer

Fueling Missions to Every Nation

I believe the growing tide of global missions and outreach can be directly tied to the exponential increase in prayer in the past one hundred years. Presbyterian pastor A. T. Pierson said near the turn of the twentieth century that "there has never been a spiritual awakening in any country or locality that did not begin in united prayer."[12] For many decades, a growing tsunami of prayer has been building in many nations. This growing focus on intercession has shown itself in many diverse forms:

- Concerts of Prayer International, started by David Bryant in the 1980s, was a revival of Jonathan Edwards's eighteenth century concept that has brought many believers together across denominational lines for days and evenings of united prayer.
- Intercessors for America, begun by John Beckett and Gary Bergel in 1975, focuses on fasting and praying for the United States the first Friday of every month. It has encouraged people around the world to start similar movements of prayer for their own nations and missions advance.
- Washington For Jesus (1980), Promise Keepers (1997), and various large Korean prayer rallies have drawn millions of people into seeking God's face for renewal and world evangelization.
- The passionate Korean church has modeled to the world a great emphasis on prayer and fasting, all-night prayer meetings, and prayer grottoes and mountains over the past sixty years.[13]

- The Polish people and their strong youth movement called OASIS met and prayed underground for decades. Many credit the fall of the Iron Curtain in 1989 to their faithful prayers.[14]
- Houses of Prayer have sprung up all over the world from Kansas City to the Mount of Olives in Jerusalem.
- 24/7 Prayer is a growing movement of youth around the world committed to radical prayer for their nations and for the lost.[15]
- See You at the Pole (SYATP) grew from a handful of students praying at their school's flag pole in a small town in Texas to encompass millions of youth in twenty-six nations for over twenty years.[16]
- Pastors Prayer Summits are now taking place around the world, encouraging pastors and Christian leaders to biblical unity and fervent intercession.[17]
- The Global Day of Prayer, started by Graham Powers, is one of the largest movements of prayer in the world today. It originated in South Africa, spread to many sports stadiums across the African continent, and went global in 2004. Millions of believers now participate annually.[18]

As the twenty-first century and its challenges move forth, the future chapter of missions history will be written with the tears and supplications of those who pray. George W. Peters believes that the history of missions abounds with evidences of divine intervention because someone prayed and God acted.[19]

Factor Three—Unity

The Lausanne Movement, AD2000, Call2All, and More

One of the greatest fruits of revival is the unifying of believers for the common cause of spreading the good news about Christ. The third wave of modern missions saw many walls break down between Christian groups and denominations that spurred the extension of the gospel worldwide.

This unifying power of the Holy Spirit took different forms, including global and localized missions conferences beginning with the World Missionary Conference held in Edinburgh in 1910. The latest *Lausanne*

Movement conference, held in Cape Town, South Africa, in October of 2010, brought together 4,500 delegates, with 70 percent of them coming from the Majority World.[20]

Christian events such as *March for Jesus* have also been used to unite believers to reach their own cultures and share the love of Jesus. Inspired by Graham Kendrick and Lynn Green in the mid 1980s, March for Jesus has brought millions of Christians together, taking to the streets not only to pray for their own towns, cities, and countries, but also to offer praise and worship to the living God.

A further step of unity in the past thirty years has been the development of various united missions movements aimed at mobilizing the church to finish the task. Luis Bush was the visionary for the *AD2000 Movement,* which held a series of global meetings in the 1990s. Its goal was "a church for every people and the Gospel for every person."[21] Bush states that "over 2000 plans have emerged independently, in country after country and around the world, and are indicators of what we must do in the years to come.[22]

The latest united thrust to reach the world via partnerships and cooperation is *Call2All.* The movement sprang out of a vision by the late Dr. Bill Bright of Campus Crusade for Christ, who wanted to reach one billion people for Christ and plant five million new churches. On August 19, 2004, a special conference brought Christian world leaders together to fulfill the vision. On December 7–8, 2004, sixty-five world leaders met in Orlando, Florida, to adopt a plan to plant five million new churches and bring a billion people to Christ. Call2All continues to hold events and workshops that target the last 639 unengaged unreached people groups in the world, representing 554 million people. The movement is growing.[23]

The prayer of Jesus in John 17 is moving forward. The evidence suggests that unity among believers will be even more universal as the twenty-first century progresses.

Factor Four—God's Providence

Migrations, Political Change, Youth, and Back to Jerusalem (BTJ)

A number of global developments greatly impacted the swelling of the evangelistic and missions tide during the twentieth century. The

Industrial and Information Revolutions enlarged the middle classes in many countries, drawing people in search of opportunity to the cities—where they came in contact with the gospel. Large people migrations, including Africans to Europe, Latinos to the United States, and Asians all over the world, brought formerly unreached people in contact with Christianity. The fall of the Iron Curtain in 1989 also exposed a large geographical portion of the world to Christian ministry and outreach.

Youth in Missions

Another significant change in the Third Wave was the mainstreaming of youth (including children) into the global missions enterprise. From the time of the early church through the first two waves of modern missions, only collegians and older adults could take up the missionary calling. In fact, during the first and second waves of missions, it was common practice for missionary families to leave their children at home or enroll them in boarding school because life in the mission field was too dangerous and disease-ridden.

Not anymore. Young children and teenagers are now vitally involved in short-term mission trips, year-round missions projects, and in fasting and praying for unreached peoples. One of the largest divisions of YWAM—King's Kids International, which began in 1976—has sent thousands of children and youth into short-term missions opportunities in over one hundred nations.[24] Many churches and missions organizations have followed suit.

The advances and specialties that were born in the twentieth century created a new and unique place for young people to join the global missions force. It started with college age young people during the Student Volunteer Movement, and progressed to include young people of all ages. The growth of youth missions around the world continues in the twenty-first century.

Majority World Missionaries

But the greatest change of the Third Wave was missionaries from the Majority World—from Africa, Latin America, the Middle East, and the rest of Asia—rising to the place of prominence in world evangelization. It was as if a torch was being passed from the west to the south and east, and this would profoundly multiply the advance of the good news.

Christianity Today ran a remarkable article in its March 2006 issue called "Missions Impossible." Beginning with an analysis of Korean missions, Rob Moll made the case that Third World missions came into their own in the last century. In 1973 there were at least 3,411 non-Western, cross-cultural missionaries in the world. That number has now exploded to 103,000, though figures are difficult to determine. That total nearly equals the number of U.S. and Canadian Protestant mission personnel, which stands at about 112,000.[25]

Yes, an explosion of Majority World missionaries is taking place around the globe. But the best is yet to come. If the Chinese Back to Jerusalem movement has its way, there may be ten million more Chinese believers added to the ranks of missions in the coming century.[26] The westward movement of the gospel, as set in motion by its Author, the Lord himself, is about to penetrate the final frontiers of Central and Western Asia and make its way back to where it all began two thousand years ago.

It's taken two thousand years for people of all nations, ages, and stations in life to take their place in global missions. Jesus told *all* of his disciples to go into all the world (Mark 16:15). It appears that *all* will finally be involved in the twenty-first century.

Factor Five—Technology

Radio, Airplanes, Vaccines, Television, Urbanization, Globalization, and the Digital Age

We have already mentioned the vast people movements that have aided world evangelization in recent decades. Michael Pocock comments:

> Historically, the spread of religions through migration may be seen in the expansion of Christianity in the first five centuries. In the year 2000, Christians of all kinds constituted one-third of the world's six billion people. During the last decades of the 1900s, the Christian movement worldwide grew by 16.4 million people a year. At the same

time an astonishing shift of the center of gravity in the non-Western world took place. . . . The pendulum has swung from a majority of the world's Christians living in the West to a majority of them now living outside it.[27]

That majority seems ready to take up the cause of world evangelization. It is a technologically sophisticated world that they are inheriting—which creates tremendous possibilities for outreach.

We discussed how the early church used the vast network of Roman roads and wide usage of the Greek language to advance the kingdom of God for centuries. During the eighteenth and nineteenth centuries, seafaring ships ferried missionaries to the coastlands of the world while advances in printing and knowledge allowed a wider distribution of the Bible and other Christian books. The Industrial Revolution brought new machinery and higher standards of living that also aided in the growth of Christian missions.

The twentieth century saw an explosion of wealth, technology, and people migration that brought an unparalleled surge in global harvest. Let's examine the tools and trends that helped caused the great acceleration in missions we've seen during the Third Wave.

First of all, modern advances in *travel*—the use of airplanes, automobiles, helicopters, missionary aviation groups, and the expanded usage of railroads and ocean-going ships—allowed access to nations in a matter of hours or days, not weeks or years. Plane travel alone birthed the growing short-term missions surge—estimated to be 540 people in 1965 and as many as four million in 2004.[28] Short-term missions trips have taken multitudes of young people to nearly every country on earth, with a portion of them returning later in life as long-term missionaries.[29]

What used to take months or years walking on Roman roads or traveling on wind-propelled ships or, later, steamships now takes a matter of hours by plane. Whereas David Livingstone traveled some 29,000 miles in his lifetime,[30] many missionaries accomplish that in a year—some in a month!

For nineteen hundred years, most people could not travel safely or widely in global missions. Today, almost anyone, at any age, can "go into all the world and preach the Good News to everyone" (Mark 16:15).

Second, the development of *modern medicine* and vaccines greatly reduced the risk of illness in traveling to other cultures and lands. Medication can be taken to combat malaria; clean water can be produced through tablets or purifiers; antibiotics heal many diseases that once led to certain death; and vaccines have halted the former plagues of polio, tuberculosis, typhoid, smallpox—even measles, mumps, and whooping cough. Many of these formerly dreaded diseases have been nearly eradicated.[31] Modern medicines enable missionaries to keep their children with them on the field and help anxious mothers and fathers release their children on short-term trips.

Third, rapid developments in *communications*—radio, television, cell phones, and the Internet—created an opportunity to reach billions of people with Christ's good news. Greater creativity during the Digital Age means that a mind-boggling amount of information is available at the fingertips of anyone who can access the World Wide Web—and this has helped the missions community raise its standard of practice and strategic engagement.

The Information Age, with its use of cable, fiber optics, computers, and microchips, has made much of the world a global village. The "JESUS" film has been seen by several billion people.[32] Young people can chat about Christ via the Internet or text their friends who may be ten thousand miles away. With computer software technology, human languages can be translated in months, not years. We live in the first period of history when every single person on earth can be reached for Christ through some form of communication.

Fourth, the *urbanization* of the world brought millions of people into cities where it is easier to reach them for Christ. The nation of Mongolia is a case in point. For centuries Mongolia had been a region of tribal groups and nomads, making it very difficult to unite and govern. When the communists came to power in the 1920s, they "created" five cities in the nation. Today nearly half of the population of Mongolia lives in Ulaanbaatar, the capital, and another third in other major cities. Whereas in 1980 there was not one known indigenous Christian believer in Mongolia, today there are fifty thousand believers and over four hundred churches. The spiritual leaders of the nation believe this can be attributed in part to evangelization in the cities.[33]

Despite the many problems associated with global urbanization, one of its benefits is the ability to share Christ's good news with millions of people.[34] Maybe this is one reason the book of Revelation pictures the future kingdom in the form of a Heavenly City—the New Jerusalem.

Finally, the reality of *globalization* has created a world culture in which people and nations are interconnected economically, socially, politically, and technologically. Though great dangers (such as tyrannical world government) could be associated with this trend, it's also true that globalization is producing a commonality among the earth's people that make them extremely open to the claims of Christ and his coming kingdom.

All of these factors—showers of revival, growing waves of prayer, a building tide of biblical unity, God's providence in raising up Majority World missionaries, and advancing technologies—produced some staggering results in global missions during the third wave of modern missions. We can't call it anything other than *amazing change*.

Chapter 9

Amazing Change

THERE IS AN EXCITING and sometimes dreaded word that characterizes the third wave of modern missions and the foreseeable future.

Change.

Many of us have experienced the birth pangs of change personally, in our families, in our vocations, or in the dizzying array of social and technological forces we encounter each day. In our modern world, if you don't change, you become relegated to obscurity.

A major reason for many of these changes is the rapid globalization of the planet. Technology has linked us together as never before, for good and for ill. From the standpoint of God's sovereign purposes, the global changes have been used for good to multiply his love.

As applied to missions, let's call it *amazing change!*

In the last two chapters we looked at the people and factors involved in the Third Wave. Now let's go deeper and analyze some of the incredible changes that occurred in missions through this Third Wave. To appreciate their magnitude, we must look at a few charts and statistics. Take your time pondering them. They tell the tale of *billions* of people hearing and responding to the good news of Jesus Christ.

The Missions Movement Becomes Global

First, let's remind ourselves of various missions movements that grew out of revival, prayer, and Christian unity over the past two millennia. Some of them are listed in table 1. Can you picture their geographical impact on world evangelization?

Table 1 Major Missions Movements AD 100 to AD 2000

1. Early Church	30–100	Mediterranean to India
2. Celtic Church	500–900	Western and Central Europe
3. Nestorian Church	450–1120	Asia
4. Orthodox Church	800–1100	Eastern Europe/Russia
5. Catholic Church	1100–1400	Northern Europe
6. Catholic Church	1500–2000	Americas, Asia
7. Russian Orthodox	1520–1680	Siberia, Alaska
8. Moravians	1730–1860	Americas, Africa
9. Protestant/Evangelical	1792–2000	Global
10. Global Evangelical		Global

Source: Patrick Johnstone, *The Church Is Bigger Than You Think* (Pasadena: William Carey Library, 1998), 70.

Notice how world evangelization began in the Mediterranean area, then began to expand. Think of these ten major mission movements as different waves that continued to extend God's message of forgiveness further around the world. They also grew in diversity as more peoples and nations joined the missionary enterprise.

Take special note of numbers 9 and 10. Today's missions force—for the first time in history—is truly global.

Evangelicals Take Center Stage

There is another interesting aspect to the latter twentieth and twenty-first century global missions enterprise. It is composed primarily of *evangelical Christians*—those who believe in the authority of the Bible and who personally share the gospel (the evangel). This is a major shift in direction.

Though other aspects of Christianity are growing, the ones in the van-guard—foretasting the emerging Fourth Wave—are *evangelical*, as shown in table 2. It depicts the ratio of world population to the number of evangelicals (360:1 in AD 100, 270:1 by AD 1000, and progressing to 9.3:1 by the year 2000).

Table 2 Growth of Evangelicals

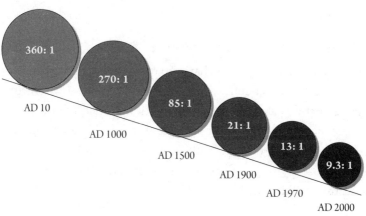

Source: Rick Wood, "Christianity: Waning or Growing?" *Mission Frontiers,* January/ February 2003, 12.

It took eighteen centuries for evangelicals to go from 0.0% of the world population to 4.5% in 1900, only 70 years to go from 4.5% to 7.1% in 1970, and just 30 years to go from 7.1% to 9.7% in 2000. This means that now, for the first time in history, there is one evangelical for every nine non-evangelicals worldwide.

Ralph Winter comments, "Despite the rapid increase in world population, the number of faithful Bible-believing Christians is increasing faster than any other large movement or religion. It is doubling every ten and a half years."[1]

One Hundred and Forty-One Evangelized Countries

Let's praise God for the incredible reversal in the status of *countries.* When William Carey, the world's first "missions statistician," published his *Enquiry* treatise in 1792, he listed over one hundred countries as virtually unreached by the gospel.[2] By comparison, in 2010, contemporary missions researcher Todd Johnson lists 141 countries as "Christian" with fifty-nine nations over half evangelized and only thirty-eight countries that are less than 50 percent evangelized.[3]

We've progressed from one hundred unreached countries in 1792 to just thirty-eight in 2010. That's an amazing change in less than 250 years!

Targeting the Remaining Unreached Peoples

There has also been significant change in evangelizing unreached peoples within the 195–267 countries or entities of the world (various groups categorize nations and territories differently). Patrick Johnstone in *The Church Is Bigger Than You Think* organizes the world's peoples in roughly thirteen thousand groupings and shows the dramatic acceleration of reaching those groups with the good news that has taken place over the past century, as illustrated in table 3.

Table 3 2000 Years of Evangelizing People Groups

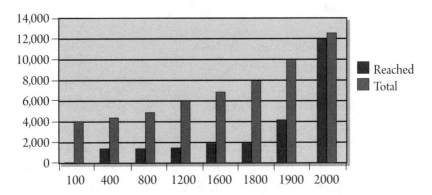

Source: Patrick Johnstone, *The Church Is Bigger Than You Think* (Pasadena: William Carey Library, 1998), 105.

Notice the tremendous uptick from 1900 to the present. The focus on hidden peoples during the Third Wave has greatly accelerated the number of tribes, tongues, peoples, and nations (ethnic groups, Greek *ethnos, ethne*) that have been introduced to Jesus Christ. For the first time in history, the goal of the Great Commission is within reach.

For example, during the past few years, *Finishing the Task* (FTT), an association of mission agencies and churches who want to see reproducing churches planted among every people group in the world, have worked in conjunction with the *Call2All* conferences to engage the remaining unreached peoples. About 2,700 of those groups have less than one hundred thousand people. *Finishing the Task* leadership identified 639 larger groups that no one was targeting. At the time of this writing, 366 of these people groups have been selected, with church planting started in 234 of them. Leaders in these movements believe the rest will be engaged in just a few short years.[4] The next task will be to enlist individuals, churches, and organizations to evangelize the remaining 2,700 smaller people groups.

The New Face(s) of Missions

Let's quantify the amazing change in *missions personnel* that has been at the heart of the third wave of modern missions. To put it simply, God's global army is changing from First Worlders (Westerners or Caucasian peoples) to those of the Majority World (developing nations in Africa, Asia, Latin America, and the Pacific—sometimes called the Two-Thirds World). During the past fifty years, Christianity's center has shifted to the Majority World, especially centered in the southern hemisphere. Rick Warren explains:

> The last fifty years has seen the greatest redistribution of a religion ever in the history of the world. For instance, in 1900, 71% of all "Christians" lived in Europe; by 2000 it had declined to just 28% who claimed to be Christian. Conversely, in 1900, only 10% of all people in Africa (10 million) were Christians vs. over 50% (360 million) today. That is a complete turnaround on a continent that's never been seen or done in history. There are by far more Christians in China than in America. There are more Presbyterians in Ghana than in Scotland. There are more Baptists in the India state of Nagaland than in the American South. There are more Anglicans in Uganda or Rwanda or

Nigeria than in England. That is a fundamental shift. If you want to know the future of Christianity, it is the developing world. It's Africa, it's Latin America, and it's Asia.[5]

Because of incredible church growth in Africa, Latin America, the Pacific, and Asia, there is a corresponding shift in those regions producing missionaries. Table 4 shows the changing dynamic of the world's *missions force* and where it is headed.

Table 4 The World's Mission Force

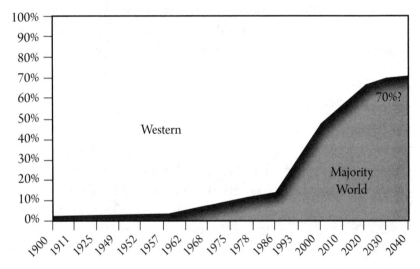

Source: Bob Waymire, LIGHT International.

The table highlights the amazing growth of Majority World missionaries in the past thirty years. Whereas very few missionaries in 1900 had been sent out from Two-Thirds World (TTW) nations, at the present time 306,000 TTW workers serve in culturally Christian nations, 103,000 TTW missionaries are sharing their faith in evangelized nations, and 10,200 TTW missionaries are doing the work of Christ in twenty-six completely unevangelized countries.[6]

Youth With A Mission (YWAM) is an example of this changing face of the global missions force. When I joined the organization in 1974,

YWAM supported three hundred full-time missionaries, 99 percent of whom were Caucasian. Today, 60 percent of the sixteen thousand full-time staff serving in 150 nations around the world are non-whites. Brazil is our second largest sending nation, and Korea is a fast rising third.[7]

This seismic change in missions personnel can also be seen in nations that were recently mission fields becoming missionary sending nations. Table 5 shows the most current statistics.

Table 5 Top Ten Missionary Sending Countries

RANK	COUNTRY	MISSIONARIES (rounded)
1	United States	127,000
2	Brazil	34,000
3	France	21,000
4	Spain	21,000
5	Italy	20,000
6	South Korea	20,000
7	Britain	15,000
8	Germany	14,000
9	India	10,000
10	Canada	8,500

Source: Todd Johnson, *The Atlas of Global Christianity* (Edinburgh: Edinburgh University Press, 2009), 310.

The face of missions is rapidly changing. Jews, Romans, Europeans, and Americans have all had their place in the history of missions. Today a new era is dawning in which people of color are taking the lead in world evangelization.

And the number of mission groups and missionaries are surging. In 1980 there were 1,800 known evangelical missionary agencies worldwide sending out 70,000 workers. Today there are 4,000 known evangelical missions groups sending out more than 250,000 missionaries from over two hundred countries.[8]

Amazing Change!

We should be thrilled about the amazing advances in Christian missions in the past two millennia—especially in the last sixty years. Many missional waves have gone forth. Scores of nations have been evangelized; thousands of people groups have been targeted and engaged. Two billion people have heard the news that Jesus can save them from their sins.

But the task is not complete. Other peoples and nations still await the power of the gospel to change their lives and futures.

It is into this tumultuous but exciting twenty-first century world that I believe the fourth wave of modern missions is emerging. It is destined to be a spiritual tsunami to bring the blessings of Christ to every family, tribe, people, and nation (Rev. 5:9).

What will the Fourth Wave look like? What will be its reach? In the final chapters I would like to suggest what God might be up to. I want *you* to find your place in the Fourth Wave.

Part 3

The Fourth Wave

"The fourth wave of modern missions will involve people of all ages and nationalities, reaching every-one in the world, using creative technologies and relational approaches, in all spheres of life, with every believer being missional."

—Ron Boehme

Chapter 10

All Ages

*The fourth wave of modern missions will involve people of **all ages** and nationalities, reaching everyone in the world, using innovative technologies and relational approaches, in all spheres of life, with every believer being missional.*

BASED ON THE ANALYSIS of past waves of missionary advance, I will suggest in the final chapters what the face of missions may look like in the twenty-first century. My projection is contained in the definition above—six trends that are already emerging, and the seventh which is the key to its ultimate success.

I'm not alone in my assessment. Jim Stier, a missions mobilizer in Brazil and the Youth With A Mission field director for the Americas, lists eight emerging characteristics of the Fourth Wave that are very similar to the above, though there is some overlap and different word choices.[1] Other additions or emphases by the Holy Spirit will be at the sole prerogative of our providential God. Only he knows the future.

The first characteristic of the fourth wave of modern missions is both unique and electrifying: for the first time in history, *people of all ages*—children, youth, families, and adults—will share a role of extending the gospel worldwide. Missions service was once the exclusive domain of adult males. Many developments and advances in history—religiously, economically, and technologically—now allow people of all age groups to participate in the Christian missionary enterprise. God is calling *all* to get involved.

Because each of us lives in one generation, we tend to view life through that particularly narrow lens. To current generations it may seem a no-brainer that people of all different ages are serving in missions around the world. But as we've discovered, this is a very recent development.

For the first nineteen hundred and sixty years of gospel outreach, the thrust of missions was populated by adults—some of them young adults, but adults nonetheless. For many of those centuries, they became adults at earlier ages, but still the difficulties of travel and rigors of living in a world with cannibals, wild animals, and without modern medicines made it nearly impossible for children and teens to engage in missional activity.

In fact, one of the wrenching problems of the first three waves was the near requirement of adult missionaries to leave their children behind in boarding schools in England, Europe, and the Americas, or erect colonial missionary compounds to protect their families from harm. Those left behind often became bitter at the loss of growing up away from their parents. Many turned their backs on a missionary career or even rejected the Lord altogether. Others felt separated and isolated in the missionary compounds and didn't develop a heart for the lost.

Dale Kauffman, an international missionary leader who founded *King's Kids International* (KKI) in 1976 to enable families to get involved in missions,[2] is typical of that era. He was born in China to missionary parents who had to flee the country following the Communist Revolution in 1948. Growing up in Japan as a missionary kid (MK), he attended boarding schools far removed from the ministry of his parents. This left him angry, disillusioned about missions, and at odds with his parents. Later on, it took a powerful move of God in his heart to forgive his dad and eventually launch Kings Kids, which stressed families being involved in missions together.

King's Kids now includes thousands of parents, teens, and children going out on summer mission teams and serving in long-term works all over the world. My own family of eight grew up in a King's Kids ministry which sent 100–150 adults, teens, and children into twenty nations from 1991 to 2001. Our kids were blessed to be born in the first era of history where youth and children could take a role in completing the Great Commission.

Being born in this generation is quite a privilege. If you were the apostle Peter's first-century child, you couldn't be involved in missions. If you were the children of many First or Second Wave missionaries in the nineteenth century, you were separated from your parents' missionary work. But if you were born in the latter part of the twentieth or the beginning of the twenty-first century, then you have the staggering privilege of being missional at a very early age. There are a number of ways to get involved. Consider the following stories from real people.

Hillary was seven years old when she heard that Chinese children needed blankets. She decided to send her treasured baby lambskin to meet the need, and motivated her friends to give financially and collect supplies for an unreached Chinese minority group. Though Hillary was just in elementary school, God used her to motivate her church to send short-term teams to China, where people were saved and many families were blessed with clothing, supplies, and playground swing sets.

Hillary is representative of many young children who are reading missionary biographies, learning about unreached peoples, and then launching projects to bring others to Christ around the world. Hillary wasn't able to go out by herself to the mission field. But she had the savvy, tenacity, and the resources of the twenty-first century to personally adopt an unreached people, raise money, and then help send teams and supplies to that group to share the good news of Jesus. Hillary was living a missional life before the age of ten.

Hanna (not her real name), was a shy fourteen-year-old who started going out on summer missions teams in 1995. During her high school years, she fell in love with Jesus and world evangelism, and then joined a team in Hong Kong following graduation. By the time she was twenty-one, she had seen thousands come to Christ in China, India, and many nations in Southeast Asia. Today she is a wife and mother of three young children, who, along with her husband, are successfully planting churches in central China. Hanna started her mission career at fourteen and has never looked back.

In the twenty-first century, millions of young children and teenagers will engage in missions. They will do it through prayer, financial support, humanitarian projects, short-term missions teams, and in families that serve together in missions. They have the information, resources, opportunities, technology, and passion to take their place in completing the Great Commission.

But *all ages* also means that people in their mid to late years can also be missionaries. In Youth With A Mission, one of the largest segments of society joining the missionary ranks are those over forty who have raised their families, are in mid-career, or simply want to use their latter years for missionary service. A number of missionary-support organizations, such as SOWERS (Servants on Wheels Ever Ready), Mission Builders, and MAPPERS, mobilize skilled people of the older generation to serve the missions cause.

Also, in YWAM one of the most popular training programs is the Crossroads Discipleship Training School (CDTS), which is designed to enable older-generation saints to live their later years on a missional trajectory. Through prayer, financial contributions, and becoming "moms and dads" and "grandpas and grandmas" on the mission field, senior saints are showing that it's never too late to be a missionary.

I have a friend named Roy who supported missions activities all his life. After his wife died in her seventies, he took a number of mission trips to use his electrical skills for Jesus. A couple of years ago, he joined a missions outreach to Mexico—at the age of ninety-five.

In the fourth wave of modern missions, there will be fewer and fewer barriers to people of all ages living a missional lifestyle. You can be involved in missions at any age. We are the first generations to share the privilege.

Chapter 11

All Nationalities

*The fourth wave of modern missions will involve people of **all** ages and **nationalities**, reaching everyone in the world, using innovative technologies and relational approaches, in all spheres of life, with every believer being missional.*

AN EXCITING BATON is being passed in God's plan for redeeming the world:

- The first "runners" in the race were Jewish people, both in ancient times and in the Early Church Wave.
- During the Middle Ages, Jews passed the baton to Gentile citizens of the Roman Empire who became the primary missionaries of the gospel for hundreds of years. This movement produced many great African leaders of the faith as well as Europeans. What linked them together was the infrastructure of the Pax Romana (Roman Peace).
- After Europe was Christianized and the Reformation brought renewal to a backslidden continent, the baton of world missions was passed primarily to European Protestants during the first wave in modern missions.

- Americans were handed the baton following the War Between the States (Civil War), and then led the world in missional focus for much of the Second Wave and all of the Third.

But as we've seen, beginning in the latter half of the twentieth century, God began to pour out his Spirit in Latin America, much of sub-Saharan Africa, and many parts of Asia, leading to a dramatic shift in the center of Global Christianity. Today the baton is clearly being passed to the Majority World nations who are destined to lead the crest of the building Fourth Wave.

The truth is this: in the fourth wave of modern missions, all nationalities will serve at the same time, being led by new participants. This is an exciting development in God's missional plans.

It is God's sovereign moment for the Majority World to lead the next or final wave in world evangelization. In the Fourth Wave, the typical missionary will not be a white First Worlder. He or she will be a person from Africa, Latin America, the Pacific Islands, the Middle East, or Asia. It is their day to arise and go forth!

The Tokyo 2010 Global Mission Consultation underlined this amazing change that is occurring in global missions. For many, the highlight of the conference was Stefan Gustavsson, leader of the Swedish Evangelical Alliance, who pleaded with the delegates to "come over and help us!" as he lamented the decline of the Christian faith in Europe. Dr. Gustavsson was echoing the call of the man in Paul's Macedonian vision almost two thousand years ago. In response to his plea, a tearful Dr. Yong Cho, a Korean who is director of the Global Network of Mission Structures (GNMS), came to the podium and the entire assembly began to cry out to God for the peoples of Europe.[1]

What an amazing turn of events! It was European missionaries who faithfully brought the good news to the Majority World peoples over the past four hundred years. In the twenty-first century, Majority World missionaries are needed to return the favor—and beyond.

Tokyo 2010 was one of four international gatherings in 2010 designed to follow up on the great Edinburgh conference of 1910. The

Tokyo gathering was typical of the changing of the guard that is taking place in world missions. Delegate David Taylor described it this way:

> An interesting feature of Tokyo 2010 that surprised many Western delegates was the number of African missionaries serving in Japan. . . . Ironically, as many older missions have been pulling their personnel out of Japan due to the high cost of living, God has been replacing them with missionaries from some of the poorest nations on earth!
>
> These African missionaries are a tiny glimpse of a seismic shift that . . . is changing the global Church and global missions movement. Dr. Yong Cho commented . . . , "The day will come when even the majority of personnel serving with international missions of Western origin will be made up predominantly of non-Western cross-cultural missionaries."[2]

Tokyo 2010 was the first global missions conference that was organized, conducted, attended, and *funded* by a majority of non-Western mission leadership. It will not be the last.

YWAM is typical of the global change that is occurring. By YWAM's fiftieth anniversary in 2010, the organization had grown to encompass people from 107 nations, with the greatest growth taking place among people of color. Our second largest nationality is *Brasileros*—dynamic young missionaries from Brazil. We have a large and growing contingency of Koreans, Indians, Nigerians, and many other Asian and African nationalities. On all our YWAM training campuses we stress both the need and desire to become totally and truly international. It is taking place before our eyes.

In 2010, YWAM was staffed by 16,000 global missionaries. Our goal is to grow to 200,000 during the next fifty years. If we are to reach that goal by God's grace, it can be said with certainty that the majority of those 184,000 new missions recruits will hail from the Majority World nations.

More specifically, I believe the greatest additions to the global missions force in the twenty-first century will come from the two largest nations on earth—China and India. Chinese Christians have a burning desire to share their faith all over the world. But their present political situation does not allow most to travel.

Sometime during this century, I believe God will initiate events that will send tens of millions of Chinese out as cross-cultural missionaries. They will follow the lead of the Korean church in taking their vision globally. They will be a welcome addition to world evangelism. Instead of just seeing Chinatowns and Chinese restaurants in many cities of the world, I believe the day will come when Chinese churches and ministries dot the landscape. The Chinese will be a significant part of the next wave.

One of the most strategic prayers we can pray in the twenty-first century is for China to be become free and send millions of missionaries all over the world with the good news of Jesus Christ.

We must also pray for India. This great nation with past British and Christian influence, though populous and poor, is emerging in the twenty-first century as a possible economic and missionary power. An alliance between Indian and Chinese Christians would be a potent combination in the coming move of God's Spirit. Let's pray fervently for God's plans to come forth for the Asian giants of China and India.

But many other nationalities in Africa, Latin America, the Middle East, and Asia are also taking their place in world evangelism. Africans are making an impact in some European nations;[3] Hispanics make up an important portion of the church that is growing in North America;[4] Muslim peoples are coming to Christ in Indonesia, Iran, and other nations.[5]

One major strategy God is using to explode his church throughout all nationalities is indigenous church-planting movements. Because of the following factors, David Garrison of the International Mission Board believes these movements cause exponential growth of disciples and churches:[6]

- Rapid—new churches start much quicker than traditionally.
- Multiplicative—the number of churches grow at an exponential rate by multiplication, not addition.
- Indigenous—they start from within the culture or population segment and don't depend on outside resources to multiply.

- Churches planting churches—ordinary church members, not professional clergy, accept responsibility for starting new churches.

Garrison believes there are ten components common to all church-planting movements: prayer, abundant gospel sowing, intentional church planting, Scriptural authority, authentic living, local focus, lay leadership, cell or house churches, churches planting churches, and rapid reproduction. These factors produce healthy churches centered on worship, evangelism, discipleship, ministry to others, and fellowship.[7]

Church planting movements are springing up in many nations. The fourth wave of modern missions will be a global wave of love, service, and good news to every nation on earth. And it will be made up of people from all nationalities and races—for the first time in history.

God's "rainbow coalition" is coming with the good news of Jesus Christ. And it is destined to touch every single person who lives on Planet Earth.

Chapter 12

Reaching Everyone

The fourth wave of modern missions will involve people of all ages and nationalities, **reaching everyone in the world,** *using innovative technologies and relational approaches, in all spheres of life, with every believer being missional.*

JESUS MEANT WHAT HE SAID when he commanded his disciples to "go into all the world and preach the Good News to everyone" (Mark 16:15).

The early church obeyed his commands and took the message of salvation to much of the Roman Empire. God's truth was advancing so triumphantly in that period that the Apostle Paul could say that "this same Good News that came to you is going out all over the world. It is bearing fruit everywhere by changing lives" (Col. 1:6).

After centuries of advance and decline during the Middle Ages, the missionary endeavor was catapulted far beyond the borders of the Roman Empire to those far corners of the world where William Carey had lamented that out of a population of 731 million, an estimated 420 million still lay in pagan darkness.[1] In Carey's day, 57.5 percent of the world's population had never heard of Jesus Christ.

In contrast, by 2010 our world population stood at 6.7 billion, a nearly tenfold increase over Carey's 1792 estimate. But the influence of the first three waves of modern missions had taken the gospel within reach of nearly 4 billion people, leaving 2.7 billion, or 40.7 percent still unevangelized. This improvement of 17 percent is great news—but not for those who are still without Christ.

It is uncertain how the world population will grow in the coming years. The estimates of the United Nations (UN) vary greatly for 2050—from a low of 7.5 billion to a high of 10.6 billion.[2] After that, the UN's 127-page report lists numerous variables that could affect population estimates in the next two hundred years, finally concluding that global population could explode as high as 36.4 billion in 2300 or sink as low as 2.3 billion.[3] Suffice it to say that the brightest minds on earth don't really know how many people will populate the planet in the near or distant future.

But God does—and he wants to share the good news of his Son with every one of them. The fourth wave of modern missions could make that possible.

Over two billion people in the world now identify themselves as Christians—making Christianity the largest faith in history. If hundreds of millions of these followers of Christ could be enlisted to pray, engage, support missionaries, and use the many forms of technology that are available to us today, then billions could hear about the love of God in a very short amount of time.

As noted in previous chapters, there are numerous global initiatives aimed at adopting, engaging, and reaching the remaining hidden peoples around the world. For example, at a recent international missions convocation, a list of 639 unengaged peoples, each with a population over fifty thousand, was presented to mission leaders and 171 of these peoples were selected by agency leaders for outreach in the next three to five years.[4] These types of commitments are becoming more and more common as Majority World missionaries join the growing Fourth Wave.

Call2All, a partnership of hundreds of the top missions agencies, denominations, and organizations in the world, is one such group that is seeing hundreds of unreached people groups targeted for evangelization in conferences around the world.[5] One strategy of the Call2All, developed by strategist David Hamilton, is *Project 4K*—an emerging paradigm of looking at the world.[6] It's a way of global mapping that divides the world into four thousand squares where towns, cities, and nations are prayed for, engaged, and evangelized.

There are four basic concepts behind Project 4K. First, it is of vital importance to have a biblical worldview that understands the importance of fulfilling of the Great Commission. Second is the call of all Christians to actively participate in taking the gospel to all people, to all places, and to all spheres of all societies. (Project 4K gets the "everyone" focus.) The third part is determining "where we are not." Jesus said, "If a man has a hundred sheep and one of them gets lost, what will he do? Won't he leave the ninety-nine others in the wilderness and go to search for the one that is lost until he finds it?" (Luke 15:4). As a very practical aspect, Project 4K uses a digitized map of the world (kind of a Christian version of Google earth) to locate where the church is *not*.

Finally, the Project 4K map contains a new approach to the use of geography. Population limits are used to reorganize existing civil divisions into a unified system of areas called *Omega Zones*. Based on the availability of the gospel in each area, different limits on population gently focus attention on where the gospel is needed the most while still including the entire world. There are three different types of Omega Zones—the "Last Places" on earth that need to receive God's love.

1. In an area where the gospel is not available (World A), the population is limited to 3 million per zone.
2. In an area where the gospel is partially available (World B), the population is limited to 6 million per zone.
3. In an area where the gospel is readily available (World C), the population is limited to 9 million per zone.

The goal of Project 4K is to engage millions of Christians worldwide in adopting an Omega Zone of the world for concentrated prayer, personal visits, mission teams, financial support, and long-term ministry. A church of 4,000 could "engage" the whole world, in some form, by every member adopting an Omega Zone. A small congregation could target one or a number of Omega Zones for concentrated intercession and outreach.

Youth groups could take on an Omega Zone. Small groups could do the same.

And individual Christians can also focus like a laser on one particular Omega Zone of the world as a lifetime passion.

I have personally adopted the Omega Zone of Mongolia and have been working there for thirteen years. I pray regularly for the nation. I take teams to Mongolia once or twice a year to engage in evangelistic projects and humanitarian needs. I have solicited grants and have helped to start businesses in this relatively poor former Soviet satellite. I've organized training sessions for pastors and youth leaders, and even used sports teams to share the gospel in this Buddhist nation.

Over the years I've been working in Mongolia, God has motivated many others to target this once totally unreached nation. When I started going to Mongolia, there were only a few thousand believers in the nation. Today there are fifty thousand in five hundred churches, and the vision of the Mongolian church leaders is to reach 10 percent of the nation by 2020. Many Mongolian Christians are now targeting their own Omega Zones around the world and doing what they can to spread the good news.

I've chosen my Omega Zone. How about you?

For the first time in history, we truly have the manpower, resources, and the know-how to reach *every single person on earth with Christ's offer of salvation.* The building wave of *his story* runs like this: from Jerusalem, to the coastlands, to the interiors, to unreached peoples, to each neighborhood, to every person.

Chapter 13

Using Innovative Technologies

*The fourth wave of modern missions will involve people of all ages and nationalities, reaching everyone in the world, **using innovative technologies** and relational approaches, in all spheres of life, with every believer being missional.*

BOTH THE INDUSTRIAL REVOLUTION and, more recently, the Information Revolution have caused a great acceleration in the pace of world evangelization. These leaps are largely due to developments in technology and communications that have taken place in the past one hundred and fifty years—something that God has providentially allowed in his orchestration of history.

It hasn't always been this way. From the time of Julius Caesar to George Washington—over eighteen hundred years—the world's main technological systems, from military strategy to agricultural techniques, changed little. But the Industrial Revolution of 1760–1850 (which included developments in agriculture, textile and metal manufacturing, transportation, economic policies, and social structures) greatly aided global missions. These innovations led to a greater ease of travel, wealth creation for missions support, and better communication to and from the mission field.

In the twentieth century, further technological advance through the invention of the automobile, telephone, radio, television, air travel, and use of medical vaccines to prevent disease has helped explode the gospel into every nation on earth. Samuel Morse's famous first words, "What hath God wrought?" on an open telegraph line between Baltimore and Washington, DC, on May 24, 1844, is certainly our exclamation today! God has allowed an explosion of scientific discovery in our lifetimes that has not only changed the world and how it operates, but has shrunk that world to very reachable dimensions.

The twenty-first century missional believer will make full use of the Information Revolution to reach every person with the good news of Christ. Let's mention just a few of the innovative technologies and strategies that are helping to point the world to Christ.

Radio

Though an older media, radio continues to dominate as a medium of missions all over the world. The Far East Broadcasting Company (FEBC) has been sharing Christ's love with Asia and the Pacific since 1952 in two hundred languages in 160 countries.[1] Trans World Radio (TWR) is the other Christian radio giant, with thirty-two transmitters located throughout the world, broadcasting in 150 languages.

Steve Shantz, TWR's chief information officer says, "I am mindful of the billions of people who will never read content in a Web browser, send a "tweet" or even read an e-mail. This demographic majority will be with us for some time, and the most effective way to reach them is through radio." Shantz is right—especially in continents like Africa where 1 in 160 people have Internet access, 1 in 130 have a computer, 1 in 35 have a telephone, but 1 in 3 have a radio.[2]

Radio is still critical to reaching people in developing nations. Lex Gerts, European Union representative, agrees that "in those parts of the world where technological development still has a long ways to go, radio has proved to be the most cost-effective and far-reaching media [*sic*]."[3] Radio's reach will only expand in the twenty-first century.

Television

I remember getting our first color TV in 1960 and watching in awe the broadcast of *The Wizard of Oz*. At that point, commercial television had only been around ten years or so. Today there are an estimated 1.4 billion television sets in the world that allow nearly 5 billion people access to news, information, and entertainment.[4]

Christian innovators like Pat Robertson's Christian Broadcasting Network (CBN) harnessed the use of television for preaching the gospel in 1961, and by 1977 had become America's first basic cable TV network. CBN is now beamed via satellite transmissions to 218 countries and territories in different languages—from Mandarin to Turkish, and Spanish to Welsh. CBN has seen millions of people come to Christ through their broadcasts and outreaches.[5]

Trinity Broadcasting Network (TBN), started by Paul Crouch in 1973, "began with a vision to build a Christian television network that spans the whole world."[6] TBN is the world's largest Christian television network, with five thousand stations and thirty-three international satellites. It is a major producer of Christian films and is on the cutting edge of technological innovation with three virtual reality theaters in three U.S. cities.

Many newer television stations and ministries are being born around the world to spread the good news on the airwaves and through charitable projects as well. GOD TV, begun in 1995 by Rory and Wendy Alec in the UK but now based in Israel, is one of the new breed of Christian television ministries. Their mission is to "reach the lost and equip believers all across the world."

While filming the aftermath of the 2004 tsunami that hit Sri Lanka, a GOD TV staffer came across a woman living in a makeshift shelter on the northeast coast of the island. Her name was Shiryawati and she had lost everything. Through GOD TV's Relief Fund, they were able to buy her a piece of ground and build her a home with electricity and running water. The home has two bedrooms, a kitchen, toilet, and shower—and a television set where she can watch GOD TV with her Muslim and Hindu neighbors. Through the use of television, others are coming to Christ.[7]

Many of us can't live without television in the modern world (from our big screens to our iPhones). This generation will use the power and reach of television to tell a world that Jesus cares and that he *saves*.

Film

Movies and films are also being used by this creative generation to complete the Great Commission. One movie in particular has led the way in sharing Christ with those who have little knowledge of him.

According to Pastor Rick Warren, author of *The Purpose Driven Life*, "The 'JESUS' film is the most effective evangelistic tool ever invented." Just about every four seconds, somewhere in the world, another person indicates a decision to follow Christ after watching the "JESUS" film, produced by a ministry of Campus Crusade for Christ. Every four seconds—that's about 21,000 people per day, 630,000 per month, and more than 7.5 million per year.

Called by some "one of the best-kept secrets in Christian missions," a number of mission experts have acclaimed the film as one of the greatest evangelistic tools of all time. Since 1979 the "JESUS" film has been viewed by several billion people (yes, BILLION!) across the globe, and has resulted in more than 225 million men, women, and children making decisions to follow Jesus. Based on the Gospel of Luke, the "JESUS" film has now been translated into more than one thousand languages, with a new language being added nearly every week. This brings God's Word to people in more than two hundred countries in languages they know and understand. By God's grace, it is yielding a spiritual harvest of unprecedented results.

Not only is the story of the "JESUS" film one of effective evangelism, but also of a powerful tool for expanding the church worldwide. In fact, according to Dr. Stephen Steele, former CEO of DAWN Ministries,

"Three quarters of all churches planted in the last decade around the world used the 'JESUS' film as part of the church planting process."[8]

Other Christian movie makers are also using the power of film to point this generation to the King of kings. *Create International* is a frontier mission communication ministry committed to producing evangelistic audiovisuals in the heart language (mother tongue), and cultural style of the people group they are created for. These resources equip workers reaching out to some of the least evangelized people groups in the world such as the Bengalis of Bangladesh, the Zhuang in China, and the Wolofs of Senegal and The Gambia.[9] They have produced scores of videos for reaching the least of the unreached.

Bollywood, India's Hindu-language film industry and the world's second largest global film maker, is also getting into the act. Millions of Indians have seen *Dayasagar,* a movie about the life of Jesus, directed by and starring Vijaya Chandar. As a result, feature-film outreach has earned its place as a powerful tool for Christians in Hindu-majority India. According to Joseph D'Souza, president of the *All India Christian Council,* "In the Indian context of multi-faith communities, propagating the story of Jesus is the wisest way to bring the people over to church. Film evangelists in India are doing the initial part of paving the ground for a personal experience of faith."[10]

In India, the world's second largest nation, *Operation Mobilization* (OM) has 140 field teams working with local churches to distribute literature and screen films. "After each show, 5 to 10 percent of viewers decide to choose Jesus as their Savior," says Kumar Swamy, director of OM's south zone. "We don't force them to change their names that identify them as non-Christians or shun their gods. In the course of time, they themselves do it." Swamy hopes to plant one thousand new churches in southern India through the use of film evangelism.[11]

Also, millions of young people all over the world are eagerly learning video and editing skills that can be used to advance the harvest. God is the author of the greatest story of all—the good news—and film is becoming one of the preferred mediums for sharing it with the world.

Orality and the Arts

Not all twenty-first century methods will be high tech. One of the fastest growing innovative strategies bursting upon the body of Christ worldwide is oral methods to reach many of the remaining hidden peoples. Learning the art of "storytelling"—and using many modern forms of technology to do it—is a critical element in the Fourth Wave.

Paul Eshleman, the founder of the "JESUS" film project and director of the Finishing the Task network states:

> I believe the subject of orality or reaching oral learners is one of the breakthrough ideas that is just starting to gain momentum. Two-thirds of people worldwide are oral learners. That is, they prefer to learn through proverbs, music, poetry, and especially stories. As mission leaders, we must re-think how we are delivering our evangelism, discipleship, and church planting strategies.[12]

The International Mission Board of the Southern Baptist Convention, one of the world's largest missionary organizations, has made a major commitment in the twenty-first century to reaching cultures that prefer oral methods of communication to the written word. Their *Orality Strategies* division believes that oral cultures work at putting every important truth or piece of information into easily-remembered forms. Proverbs are pithy, memorable ways of storing truths. Poems and songs are often easier to remember than simple lists of truths or facts.

Oral cultures develop standard ways of structuring proverbs, poems, and stories. Those patterns of organizing spoken language for ease in recall and presentation are also part of orality. Wise missionaries understand that if they want an oral culture to understand a message, it would be helpful to present it in forms that are familiar to them. That understanding helps them find the best way to present the Bible's message so they can understand it, retain it, benefit from it, and pass it on to others.[13] Many native cultures are avid oral learners such as the Sudanese cattlemen, rebel soldiers in the Congo, and the Patuas of India.[14]

Have you noticed how the young generation, now coming of age, are extremely arts-oriented in their preferences and desires? They love music, visuals, dance, drama, mime, artistic expressions, and good storytelling shared in many creative forms. Could it be that God is preparing a global generation of youth to become the best oral storytellers the world has ever known?

I believe that he is, and that orally they will present "The Greatest Story Ever Told" to a waiting world.

The Digital Age

Computers, the Internet, and Mobile Technologies

I wrote my first book in 1976 on a manual typewriter. It was a laborious process and extremely difficult to edit or correct. However, it was a vast improvement from being a monk in the tenth century who often took months or years writing a precious manuscript by hand.

In 1983 I bought my first home computer for $3,000 (nearly $8,000 in today's dollars). It was bulky, slow, and had very little memory. I'm typing away today on a laptop that cost $500, has one hundred times the speed and memory of my original machine, and can connect to a digital highway called the Internet that instantly connects me to billions of resources all over the world.

Certainly the greatest technological innovations of the current era have been the invention of the computer, the creation of the global Internet, and the increasing use and popularity of mobile devices, especially cell phones.

These incredible inventions—the hallmark of the Digital Age—are changing the world on every level and linking us together, for good or for worse, as a global village. Digital media have transformed the world in the last fifteen years. We have entered a "digital communication culture" where all the rules for effective communication have changed.

Take cell phones for example. There are about three billion mobile phone users in the world today, equivalent to 48 percent of the world's population. There are more mobile phones used in Africa than the United States. The mobile systems in Japan and Korea are highly advanced. Unlike a computer, a mobile is always with you—an integrated part of you and your lifestyle.[15]

There has been a striking convergence between the capabilities of different types of mobile devices. Although base-level phones are still available, devices increasingly offer a range of functions way beyond phone calls and text messaging. These include e-mail, web browsing, MP3/video player, radio/TV reception, global positioning and maps, buddy location and parental child-monitoring, still/video camera, games console, book reading, word processing, barcode scanning, e-ticketing, diary/planner and appointment reminder, WiFi connectivity, and Bluetooth capability.

By 2020 experts predict that the majority of web access will be via mobile devices. In the mobile arena, developments are proceeding at lightning speed. Desktop PCs and laptops are much the same as five years ago (just a bit faster with more memory), but mobile devices and applications are advancing month by month. What will the mobile world look like by 2020? Pew Internet suggests that mobiles will be more computer than phone.[16]

This incredible technological revolution is a phenomenal opportunity for reaching every person on earth with the message of salvation. Through phone calls, Skype, text messaging, chat rooms, forums, social networking, and tweets, the people of the world can learn about Jesus and come into a saving relationship with him.

For example, Wycliffe Bible Translators (WBT) is greatly speeding up the work of Bible translation because of the power of computing. There are 6,909 spoken languages in the world. With the old Wycliffe motto being "one team, one language, one lifetime," the organization believed it could finish the task of translating at least a portion of the Bible into every spoken language by 2150.

But portable computers and satellites are speeding things up by about 125 years. Previously, a Wycliffe missionary family or team would spend decades learning and transcribing one language in a remote corner of the earth. But because of technological advances, Bible translators will have at least some of the Bible written in every one of the world's spoken languages by 2025. Paul Edwards, leader of Wycliffe's Last Languages Campaign says, "We're in the greatest period of acceleration in two thousand years."[17] That's one of the blessings of the Digital Age.

The technological explosion impacts us daily. For example, this week was typical for me—a baby-boomer with moderate user skills. I typed fifty pages on a laptop and sent out two blogs that went to hundreds of people around the world. While shooting hoops with my son outside our home, I received a text message from a young African in Liberia to arrange future ministry. One evening I encouraged a Mongolian disciple as we chatted on Skype (with a perfect picture!). I used the GPS application on my cell phone for an appointment concerning a missions project halfway around the world and messaged my son in Los Angeles who was doing a video shoot near Hollywood.

If my generation can learn to navigate the digital age to this limited degree, imagine what younger generations growing up in this digital world will be able to accomplish for Christ during the remainder of this century. I believe billions of people will hear about Jesus through digital technology in the coming years. It will be the greatest evangelism explosion in the history of the world.

Pastor Joel Hunter of the Northland Church in Orlando, Florida, says, "I can tell you that this is one of the most exciting things I have ever been a part of in my forty years of ministry. God is inviting us to be a part of something that is simply amazing!"[18] He's talking about the possibilities of sharing Christ in the Digital Age.

Global Media Outreach, a division of Campus Crusade for Christ, has developed over one hundred websites dedicated to this task. Using the Internet as a communication platform, people can chat, pray, and learn about Jesus with caring people thousands of miles away. Global Media Outreach saw ten million people make decisions for Christ in 2009.[19] This is certainly the future wave of missions.

Digital wonders will also be used to globally map the final horizons of world evangelization. *Last Mile Calling* is a global partnership that is preparing a "Global Church Planting Database" system. This tool will enable national websites to be built in local languages, showing the progress of church planting in every village and town, using a central mapping service. The creators of this software are telling Christian leaders, "Tell us what you need and we'll build it."[20]

In the days when the tabernacle was being built, God anointed some men with "wisdom, ability, and expertise" to help get the job done (Exod. 31:3). Could today's Christian computer programmers and engineers be the modern-day equivalent of such men who will help the Lord build a global "house" made up of all people?

Today's generations are technologically savvy and are being prepared to share the news about Jesus through innovative inventions far more powerful than anything the world has ever seen. A new wave of salvation needs new tools to power it. The May 2010 Tokyo Declaration contains these challenging words: "God has entrusted this generation with more opportunities and resources to complete the task than any previous one. We have more mission-minded churches, more sending structures and bases, more missionaries, more material resources, more funding, more and better technology, more information and data, a deeper understanding of the task, and a clearer focus of our responsibility than previous generations. God will require much of our generation."[21]

The technocrats of Jesus are coming. Though preaching and teaching will always be a part of sharing God's Word, the most artsy and communication-oriented generation of all time will make use of a wide array of methods and tools to fill the earth "with the knowledge of the glory of the Lord" (Hab. 2:14 NKJV).

But they will do so through the means of relationships—because that's what an anxious and broken world so desperately needs.

Chapter 14

Relational Approaches

*The fourth wave of modern missions will involve people of all ages and nationalities, reaching everyone in the world, using innovative technologies and **relational approaches**, in all spheres of life, with every believer being missional.*

RELATIONAL MINISTRY—both through the use of technology and face-to-face—will be the norm in the Fourth Wave. There are a number of reasons why friendship evangelism—personal, one-on-one, heart-to-heart sharing of the good news—is here to stay and will prevail in the twenty-first century.

Relational focus is partly due to the shift in missionary personnel. For most of history, missionary outreach was made up primarily of men, who tend to do more formal and structured activities than women and youth. Today's missional force is made up primarily of women, who are highly relational in their approach to sharing their faith, and it is increasingly incorporating youth and children, who have the same operating style. The other factor is the shift to the Majority World peoples living mainly in the southern hemisphere and large portions of Asia. Most of these cultures are very hospitality and relationship oriented—especially compared to European and North American cultures. They will bring their cultural strengths into the advance of world missions.

Second, the age of television has created an increasingly informal, high-touch world where formal structures are seen as stiff and outdated. Evangelism has always adapted to these cultural changes. For example, Western culture of the eighteenth and nineteenth centuries was very structured due to the influence of Puritan and Victorian standards—and the missionaries of that era shared the same tendencies. *The Salvation Army,* which began in 1865 and was first called the East London Christian Mission, was born in a time where disciplined, marching armies were the admired norm. It was natural and culturally relevant for the William and Catharine Booth to demand that their missionaries wear military type outfits and change their name to "Salvation Army" to fit the time period. The nineteenth century loved "armies," so God's workers followed suit.

One hundred years later, television has brought individual narratives and real-life family dramas into the homes of the average person. The first television shows were fairly stiff, but over time as interviews were done on comfortable chairs in living room sets, the atmosphere of informality began to prevail. The advent of reality shows, where people are seen and heard in their sometimes crude and natural environments, is an even stronger statement of relational informality. Two generations have now been raised in this increasingly close-to-home and informal world. It's where they live, the shows they watch, and the music they enjoy.

The modern church has struggled to adapt to this increasingly informal world. Many churches have fought the move from the straight-back pews to padded pews and then to more versatile moveable chairs. The sanctuary was once viewed as a holy place to be treated with awe and silence. Today it can double as a basketball court on weekends and an *AWANA* games circle during the week. Espresso stands are common, and pastors now teach and preach (actually "talk" and "share"), not from formal pulpits, but with lecterns, bar stools, and in living room settings—sometimes with a drama, skit, or personal narrative thrown in. Creative, relational informality is king in the twenty-first century.

This is part of an overall trend where the church is being de-institutionalized to be effective in our highly social, relational world. It appears that denominations and structures are out; networking and cooperation are in. Though some churches are seeing a renewal of traditional forms or liturgy, a larger segment is modernizing to remain relevant in our laid-back world of burgeoning social networks.

The youth of this era know no other culture. They grew up on *Friends* and *Oprah*, MySpace and Facebook—and are drawing their parents and grandparents in as well. A dominant youth idiom of the past twenty years, with amazing staying power, is the phrase "hanging out." Youth enjoy just being together. Friendships are where it's at. In today's world, hanging out can be in person, through texting, talking on cell phones, on Skype, in chat rooms, and through many other mediums that are relationship-based.

GodRev.com is one of hundreds of websites—destined to become thousands in the Fourth Wave—created to relationally touch the lives of people all over the world and pray for their growth. Their site allows you to "see" real-time conversions being made all over the world as people pray and chat with each other.[1]

Two high-tech, high touch (close and personal) missional stories follow.

Matt's Story

Matt Rich lives in Cumbria, UK, and leads The Internet Mission. He encourages and trains part-time volunteers to use the Web for evangelism, with a particular emphasis on sharing in chat rooms and bulletin boards.

I first became involved in using the Internet for evangelism whilst working as a missionary to school children. The Internet gave me a way to be able to be in contact with the young people when they were alone and weren't feeling under pressure from their friends. One day when I was praying about whether to continue with this work, I became aware that the Lord was giving me a new missionary vision—to reach out to people using the Internet. Four years ago *The Internet Mission* was launched, and I have been working full time as an Internet Missionary since then.

A number of people are associate e-vangelists with the mission and they use the Internet for evangelism in many different ways—websites, e-mail, discussion boards, etc. Most of my work is either speaking to people in the chat rooms of the Internet or answering questions that people ask me through our website *Why Believe*. As a mission, our aim is to expand the work so that we can become more effective in reaching out to more people. One of our latest projects is "Letter to You" which is a flash movie gospel presentation in the form of a letter from Jesus to the viewer. At the end of the presentation the viewer is given an opportunity to write to us the letter they would like to write back to Jesus. We have had some very good responses from this online evangelistic project.

One of the things that we have discovered is that people may feel too inhibited to talk face to face, but they are often happy to talk about their thoughts and feelings online. I personally have had long, in-depth conversations about Jesus with people in many countries including Egypt, Iran, China, India, and the USA. It is particularly exciting when you can see that God is at work in someone's life, causing them to want to be in contact to ask more and more questions.[2]

Nathalie's Story

Nathalie supervises the online mentoring for Top Chrétien's outreach websites, based in Paris.

While I was living in Paris, my heart burned for people around the world living their lives without knowing Jesus. As I was reading stories of missionaries, I felt called to become a missionary myself. One day, after an evening service, the soft and loving voice of the Lord whispered to me through the voice of my pastor: "You don't have to go abroad to be a missionary because all the nations are in Paris."

Eight years after that evening service, I could not imagine how real this word would become in my life. I am now involved in Internet Evangelism and work in full-time ministry. Through the Internet, I have been able to see thousands of decisions for Jesus every minute from all over the world.

Our Internet evangelism tool is called *Knowing God*. It exists in seven languages. Our vision is to develop the website into twenty-eight languages over the next six years, in order to reach 250 million visitors by the year 2020. My responsibility on the team is to supervise the one hundred and three counselors in France, who follow up on those needing help or asking questions about faith and God.

I encourage and serve these faithful men and women who give a large part of their time to counseling. I even follow up on enquirers myself. Up to now, I have mainly been involved in one-to-one contact. Even though I am not very skilled on the computer, that is to say not so technically talented, I enjoy sharing online or reading many encouraging testimonies. I say, "It's worth it to stay in France and see one life at a time touched and changed."[3]

Millions of people like Matt and Nathalie will be using the wonders of modern-relational technology to reach people with Christ's good news in the coming years. God will harness the closeness that the media has engendered and use it to reach other people—as friends—for Jesus.

Finally, another reason for the emphasis on close, loving relationships is the world into which the current generations were born. This is a broken and wounded generation, scarred by divorce, wars, and natural disasters. They are victims of family breakdown, have lost parents because of AIDS (primarily in Africa but elsewhere as well), and are depleted by nearly one billion abortions worldwide in the past forty years.[4] This brokenness, especially of family life, has created a deep yearning for close, interconnected friendships and the sense of worth and security that they bring.

Out of this relational longing has come a twofold generational cry for both *justice* for those who have been abandoned, broken, exploited, and oppressed, and *mercy and grace* for the hurting. The emerging church of the twenty-first century is beginning to tap into the heart of God on these subjects in very practical ways. "Justice" ministries are the number one focus on many college campuses, and numerous churches have begun to serve the poor and needy in their localities and also around the world. There is nothing more high-touch than rescuing people from the chains of injustice and showering them with the love and mercy of Jesus.

The needs of the twenty-first century will demand an explosion of personal, relational, up-close, mercy-and-justice oriented outreach to the hurting and lonely of the planet. I believe God has especially prepared this generation of children and youth for this immense task.

A worried, broken, and interconnected world needs a friend, not an institution or organization. The multicolored friends of Jesus are coming—into every sphere of life.

Chapter 15

In All Spheres of Life

*The fourth wave of modern missions will involve people of all ages and nationalities, reaching everyone in the world, using innovative technologies and relational approaches, **in all spheres of life**, with every believer being missional.*

FOR A NUMBER OF YEARS I preached an incomplete gospel. I didn't give Jesus his proper place nor rightly represent God's desires for the nations.

An encounter with two women in 1977 changed all that. Here is the story as recounted in my 1989 book *Leadership for the 21st Century: Changing Nations Through the Power of Serving*:

> In the summer of '77, I flew into San Francisco to spend a few hours with two middle-aged women who were historians. On the trip across town from the airport, I was drenched by the rain while trying to scramble to get transportation during a city-wide taxi strike. Bedraggled and soaked to the skin, I finally arrived at their lovely home in a quaint part of that beautiful city. Like two mother hens, my hostesses, Miss Verna Hall and Miss Rosalie Slater,[1] ushered me into their home, gave me a towel to dry off with, and then proceeded to fix a lovely evening meal where we chatted and got acquainted.

After the food and fellowship, they began to show me around their home, which was a stunning collection of antique furniture, beautiful decor, breathtaking art, and loads of books! In every room Verna and Rosalie would give me a free lecture on aspects of America's history and heritage as seen through the artifacts, writings, and memorabilia that they had painstakingly collected. I was fascinated by their presentation and marveled at their wisdom. After this had gone on for about 45 minutes or so, Verna turned to me, and began to ask me several pointed questions. One of them I will never forget.

"Ron," she said sweetly, and without apparent pretense, "Can you tell me why our Christian missions work in Africa, though extensive in nature, has left the majority of Africans still living in poverty, and under the domination of authoritarian governments?"

Taken back by the question, I struggled to come up with an answer. It was true that extensive missions work had been done in many African nations. In fact, a large part of the African continent was more Christianized than Europe. Yet it was also true that most African nations were still very backward when it came to economic development, and most of them possessed very harsh and unstable governments.

Why were they still living in poverty? Why were their governments so authoritarian and cruel? I didn't have the foggiest idea. Shouldn't their Christian faith have led them into aspects of economic blessing and governmental liberty? Surely their faith should have made a difference in their lives upon the earth.

I answered weakly that I didn't know. Verna did not keep me in ignorant suspense. Warmly and confidently (as if it had all been planned), she gave me the answer: "The reason so many African Christians, and many other evangelized peoples of the world today, are still living in poverty and under oppression," Verna explained, "is that the missionaries gave them an incomplete gospel. They saved their souls and didn't teach them to apply their faith to every dimension of life. They didn't serve them by teaching them to make Jesus the Lord of all of life. So they left them to live under misery and cruelty."

I was stunned by the answer. An incomplete gospel? Verna continued her motherly lecture as we moved through other rooms of the house, with Rosalie picking up where Verna left off. After a final chat while seated on the living room couch, I thanked them for their graciousness and for their time, and made my way to my next destination.

Something within me had become very unsettled. What was the calling of Christian missions? Hadn't Jesus commanded us to go into all the world and win souls for Him? After listening to Verna and Rosalie, that perspective seemed to be lacking in depth and perspective. Was the message of the gospel broader than just the saving of the individual soul? What *were* we called to do when being sent into the nations of the earth?

At that moment, and after that little divine encounter, I set my heart to answer that question. An answer had to be found. After all, I was a missionary.[2]

Jesus and the Kingdom

That answer has emerged over the past few decades through a fresh understanding of the lordship of Christ and the kingdom of God.

The older I get and the more time I spend in God's Word, the more comprehensive the scope of Christ's lordship appears. For much of our lives, many of us have believed that Christ's salvation was limited to individual souls who would come to the Savior. Deep down in our hearts there hasn't been the faith to believe that cities and nations could be impacted and changed through the teachings of Jesus Christ.

On the other hand, history records that the spread of the gospel once transformed Europe, helped give rise to modern science, greatly shaped the concept of human rights and free societies, and contributed to the growth of the middle class and free enterprise economics in European and other nations.[3] It also gave birth to a Christian-based society in America that is now being exported all over the world and is producing some of the same results. John Micklethwait and Adrian Wooldridge (one an atheist and the other a believer) make a strong case in *God Is Back:*

How the Global Revival of Faith is Changing the World that one of the most important trends of the twenty-first century is the surge in Christian faith and freedom worldwide. They say:

> Religion (Christianity) and modernity are going hand in hand, not just in China, but throughout much of Asia, Africa, Arabia, and Latin America. It is not just that religion is thriving in many modernizing countries; it is also that religion is succeeding in harnessing the tools of modernity to propagate its message. The very things that were meant to destroy religions—democracy and markets, technology and reason—are combining to make it stronger. God is back.[4]

Actually, he never left. Many Christians throughout history who understood the unique, divine supremacy of Jesus Christ have obeyed the command to bring his lordship and wisdom into everyday life. The early church transformed many aspects of Roman culture and started the first hospitals and ministries of compassion; Christian scholars began the first universities during the Middle Ages; and John Calvin and the Swiss Reformers transformed Geneva into a Christ-centered city during the sixteenth century.[5] Loren Cunningham points out in *The Book That Transforms Nations* that Norway, Korea, Fiji, and many other countries have been impacted spiritually, socially, and economically through Christians bringing the good news into various dimensions of life.[6]

Jesus himself told his followers: "All authority has been given to Me in heaven and on earth. Go therefore and make disciples of all the nations, baptizing them in the name of the Father and of the Son and of the Holy Spirit, teaching them to observe all things that I have commanded you; and lo, I am with you always, even to the end of the age" (Matt. 28:18–20 NKJV). He also told them to pray "Your Kingdom come, your will be done on earth as it is in heaven" (Matt. 6:10 NKJV).

According to these passages, the kingdom of God is *not just* a future place. Jesus is the King of that kingdom *now* and has all authority in heaven and on earth. He wants his loving will to be done as much as possible on earth as in heaven (to bless and benefit people). And he wants us to teach and disciple all nations.

Discipling Nations

Another Matthew—Matthew Henry—a respected biblical commentator and Presbyterian minister in the late seventeenth and early eighteenth centuries, gave this lofty view of the Great Commission:

> What is the principal intention of this commission; to disciple all nations, to do your utmost to make the nations Christian nations . . . to go and disciple them. Christ the Mediator is setting up a kingdom in the world, bringing the nations to be his subjects; setting up a school, bringing the nations to be his scholars; raising up an army for carrying on the war against the powers of darkness; enlisting the nations of the earth under his banner. The work which the apostles had to do was to set up the Christian religion in all places, and it was an honorable work; the achievements of the mighty heroes of the world were nothing to it. They conquered the nations for themselves and made them miserable; the apostles conquered them for Christ and made them happy.[7]

What a concept—discipling or teaching whole nations. Or seeing whole nations influenced and changed through the power of Christ's good news. Isaiah had seen this prophetic view when he exclaimed, "Arise, shine; for your light has come! And the glory of the Lord is risen upon you. For behold, the darkness shall cover the earth, and deep darkness the people; But the Lord will arise over you, and His glory will be seen upon you. The Gentiles shall come to your light, and kings to the brightness of your rising" (Isa. 60:1–3 NKJV).

What an expanded view of the role of the church on earth! God wants his light—found in the person, salvation, and teachings of Jesus Christ—to transform neighborhoods, cities, and countries. Those changes will never create heaven on earth—but can substantially point us in the right direction. Following Jesus' death and resurrection, the authority of God to accomplish this task fully rested upon the Lord. He commanded his disciples to go out and make disciples of all the nations, teaching them *all* that Jesus had commanded them. The practical effect of this would be to bring whole nations under his influence and liberating power. It wasn't just individuals that were to be saved. Whole nations could be enriched and set free through the power of his life-giving Spirit.

The current emphasis on the lordship of Christ, the kingdom of God, and discipling nations is a welcome revival of truth that many are rediscovering. Darrow Miller has written two books on the subject, *Discipling Nations: The Power of Truth to Transform Cultures,* which gives the theology of Christian nation-changing, and *LifeWork: A Biblical Theology for What You Do Every Day,* which stresses the personal importance of all believers using their God-given gifts with missional, nation-changing concentration.[8] Vishal Mangalwadi, of Indian birth, tells us in *Truth and Transformation: A Manifesto for Ailing Nations* that it is time for the church to recover and unleash the power of the good news to transform the brokenness of our times.[9]

In the late 1980s and early 1990s, Dominion Press produced a nine-volume *Biblical Blueprint Series* on applying the Christian worldview to many arenas of life. More recently, Youth With A Mission has produced a comprehensive book on the subject entitled *His Kingdom Come: An Integrated Approach to Discipling the Nations and Fulfilling the Great Commission.*[10] Organizations like *DAWN Ministries* and *Call2All* are helping believers apply these principles in their personal lives.[11]

The life and teaching of Jesus Christ have done more to change the world over the past two thousand years than any other influence in history. As Micklethwait and Wooldridge point out, that trend should continue in the twenty-first century if the church re-centers its life and mission around the supremacy of Jesus and centrality of his kingdom.[12]

The Domains or Spheres of Society

In the summer of 1975 the founder of Youth With A Mission, Loren Cunningham, was spending time with his family in a cabin in Colorado. He used the days to seek God and pray for future direction.

One day he was impressed with an idea of how to engage all Christians in mission work. A list of seven points, which would later be known as the *seven spheres of society,* came together into his mind. He believed God was giving him these categories to help the church understand its mission in influencing nations. He wrote down the ideas on a little slip of paper and put it in his pocket.

The next day Loren and his wife, Darlene, met with Bill and Vonette Bright, the founders of Campus Crusade for Christ. During the meeting, Bill started telling Loren several ways God was showing him to change a nation. Dumbfounded, Loren listened as Bill talked about the areas of society that influenced the life of a country. Loren pulled the little piece of paper out of his pocket and showed it to Bill. The lists were almost exactly the same.[13]

This understanding of the leadership spheres or domains of society has been refined since that summer. It now includes the following categories:

- Family
- Religion
- Education
- Media (Public communication)
- Celebration (including the arts, entertainment, and sports)
- Economy (business, science and technology)
- Government

The leadership domains of society have not been broadly understood by the church at large in history. In the past few years, that has begun to change, and as we advance in the twenty-first century, this area is destined to become one of the most important pillars of modern evangelism and missions.

How do you change a nation? Through understanding the various spheres of society that exist in human culture, and how these different spheres operate independently and collectively. Let us take a look at this important area that we will refer to as *sphere sovereignty*.

Sphere Sovereignty

In Romans 13, verses 1 and 2, Paul gives us the following perspective: "Let every soul be subject to the governing authorities. For there is no authority except from God, and the authorities that exist are appointed by God. Therefore, whoever resists the authority resists the ordinance of God, and those who resist will bring judgment on themselves" (NKJV).

In this passage Paul is talking about a basic fact of life, that God has established many authorities, or spheres of leadership, in human societies. There is not one authority. There are many authorities. These have all been established by God's "ordinance" and wisdom, and are obviously necessary for order and control. The Romans 13 passage mentions the established authority of civil governments—but it is in the context of God being the author of various spheres of authority.

All through the Bible, and in our everyday experience, we recognize the reality of multiple spheres of influence or authority. We see the supreme authority of God. We are told of the heavenly authority of the angels. We recognize the authority of the individual, in various talents, graces, and giftings. On earth we are well acquainted with parental authority, the authority of the church, and the various levels of civil government, from the local school board to national governing bodies. We are also familiar with many other influential areas in society such as the media, the arts, business and commerce, education, and the like.

These various societal spheres of authority are unique and independent, but also blend together to form the tapestry of human culture. The sovereignty of God reigns above them all, yet to all of them we owe a specific honor, respect, or obligation. To understand life clearly is to discern these different spheres and their relationships to one another under God. If we relate to them and live within them according to God's design, these many individual spheres become the supports of order, freedom, and blessing.

Guillaume Groen van Prinsterer of the Netherlands, a devout Christian thinker and politician in the early to mid nineteenth century, was the first to use the phrase "souvereiniteit in eigen sfeer"—*sovereignty within its own sphere*—with respect to the multiple authorities of life. His perspective was predominantly the relationship between the spheres of church and state.[14]

He had a great burden for education and held many high posts in government. However, during his lifetime he was basically a general without an army, and it was left to a spiritual protégé to fully develop and broaden the concept. That successor was Abraham Kuyper.

Kuyper was not only a great thinker but also a statesman, serving in parliament for a number of years and as prime minister of the Netherlands from 1901 to 1905; a journalist—he was editor of the daily newspaper *De Standaard* for over forty years; an educator—he founded the Free University in Amsterdam in 1880 and entitled his opening address on October 20, 1880, "Sovereignty in the Individual Spheres of Life"; a pastor and theologian in the Dutch Reformed Church; and a voluminous writer, who authored numerous books over a span of fifty years.

What was Kuyper's guiding motivation? In his own words:

> One desire has been the ruling passion of my life. . . . It is this: That in spite of all worldly opposition, God's holy ordinances shall be established again in the home, in the school, and in the State for the good of the people; to carve as it were into the conscience of the nation the ordinances of the Lord, to which the Bible and creation bear witness, until the nation pays homage again to God.[15]

Kuyper believed that all of life was under the authority of God and the lordship of Jesus Christ. He taught that Christ came to earth to redeem *all* aspects of the fall, including the elements of human society and culture. He said, "I discovered that the Holy Scripture does not only cause us to find justification by faith, but also discloses the foundation of all human life, the holy ordinances which must govern all human existence in Society and State."[16]

It was Abraham Kuyper who began to expand with great authority and practicality the concept of "sovereignty in the individual social spheres," which he generally broke up into seven different areas. In all these spheres, state government cannot impose its laws, but must reverence the innate laws of life. God rules in these spheres, just as supremely and sovereignly as he exercises dominion in the sphere of the state itself, through his chosen magistrates.

Here's the important concept: God is the Supreme Sovereign, and all other authority is *delegated* by him. On earth, there are various jurisdictions of leadership or authority, all of which are responsible directly to God, and were designed to operate independently and in complementary unity. The state, or civil government, is where officials or magistrates are to operate according to God's principles of justice (Romans 13). But there are spheres of life that are to be completely independent of state authority, yet accountable to God.

The Seven Spheres of Society

Christ and his kingdom being lived out in all the seven spheres of society will be one of the burning passions of the Fourth Wave. The latest wave of missional leaders and recruits will not limit their activities to saving souls. They will bring Christ's full message of salvation and deliverance to every area of human life. Here is a graphic of the seven spheres they will penetrate:

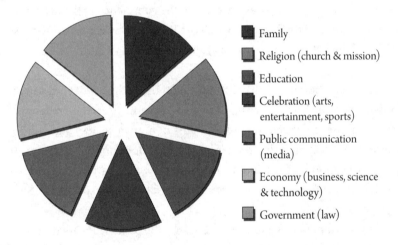

■ Family

■ Religion (church & mission)

■ Education

■ Celebration (arts, entertainment, sports)

■ Public communication (media)

■ Economy (business, science & technology)

■ Government (law)

Source: Stuart Simpson, www.thefourthwave.org

Landa Cope, director at the University of the Nation's Template Institute in Burtigny, Switzerland, who also had a jarring wake-up on God's desire to disciple nations,[17] gives the following description of the purpose of the seven spheres:[18]

Family. The purpose of family is to provide a safe, nurturing environment for growth, values, and development of the next generation. It is the smallest building block of human society. Great issues include: love, discipline, modeling God's thinking, preparation for vocation of the children, and the husband's love setting the tone of the home.

Religion (church and mission). The ecclesiastical order is called to represent God to the world and provide for the discipleship of all believers in the whole nature and character of God and his Word applied to their work and walk of faith. They are to facilitate the expression of that faith in the worship and sacraments of the church, and to be a moral model of God's absolute standards of truth.

Education. To provide for the development of the God-given gifts in every child for the service of their fellow man and society, believing every child is gifted by God and has the right for those gifts to be developed to their highest potential. Great issues include: value-based integrated process with family involvement and support.

Celebration (arts, entertainment, sports). To provide rest, relaxation, and restoration of the soul through beauty and joy.

Public communication (media). To provide truthful, objective information of importance to the community-at-large so that citizens can make informed decisions.

Economy (business). To develop an economy where needed goods and services are provided for the community along with gainful employment at a fair market price and wage. Great issues include: honest gain, enablement of the poor, integrity of the workforce, stewardship of resources, and community conscience.

Economy (science and technology). To discover and use God's laws for the blessing of all people, pursuing a higher standard of living, better health, and better stewardship of all God's natural resources. Great issues include: prevention of disease, discovery, and stewardship.

Government. To provide and ensure justice and equity for all citizens including executive, judicial, military, law enforcement, and central community services. Great issues include: justice for the weak and voiceless in society including children, women, and immigrants.

The fourth wave of modern missions will see millions of people use their gifts and talents to lift up Jesus in the seven spheres and advance his kingdom in the nations of the earth. All vocations will be viewed as *mission conduits*. There will be no such thing as professional missionaries and ordinary Christians.

In this building move of the Holy Spirit:

- Missional believers will live the teachings of Christ in their families, view homemaking as a vital mission, and work to rebuild the family unity in nations and cultures where it is broken and dysfunctional. *Christ is Lord of families.*
- In the church, the priesthood of all believers will be emphasized again as fivefold missional church leaders (modern-day apostles, prophets, evangelists, pastors, and teachers) train their people to be salt and light at every job site and in every endeavor (Eph. 4:11–13; Matt. 5:13–16). The church will speak prophetically to all the great issues of the day and lead the world in compassion and caring for the broken. *Christ is Lord of the church.*
- Missional teachers will use the realm of education to link students with their God-given destinies and teach them his wisdom and ways. Education will once again be based in the home where parents oversee the intellectual and moral training of their children. *Christ is Lord of education.*
- Missional dancers, artists, photographers, movie makers, storytellers, and athletes will use the wonderful realm of celebration to magnify the beauty and magnificence of God and point people to their Creator. All forms of artistic and athletic prowess will be seen as missional talents to encourage people. *Christ is Lord of celebration.*
- Missional businesspeople and workers will see their vocations as a divine calling where doing their best points back to Christ. Scientists will use their skills and wisdom to glorify their Maker and unwrap his secrets for the benefit of people. Doctors and nurses will see their practice as a divine calling to heal both bodies and minds. The economic policies of nations will reflect God's principles. *Christ is Lord over economics.*

- Missional government leaders at all levels will view themselves as God's representatives to impartially dispense justice and the rule of law. Emergency response professionals will view their vocations as protecting the front lines of people's God-given rights. Soldiers will defend liberty against its many adversaries. *Christ is Lord over government.*

The missionaries of the Fourth Wave will see no division between the sacred and the secular. They will view all of life as under God's authority and in need of the love, grace, wisdom, and blessing that comes from following Jesus. Their motive will be to serve as he did. They will do so, not within the confines of a sanctuary or temple, but on every person's street and in every person's town.

In doing so, whole nations and cultures can be changed through the power of the Holy Spirit. Every individual will not be saved, because that is a matter of personal choice, and many will choose the broad path of destruction (Matt. 7:13). But whole tribes and countries will experience the salt and light of the awakened mission-minded church.

The friends of Jesus are coming into every sphere of life. The key to that tidal wave is every believer becoming missional.

Chapter 16

With Every Believer Being Missional

The fourth wave of modern missions will involve people of all ages and nationalities, reaching everyone in the world, using innovative technologies and relational approaches, in all spheres of life, **with every believer being missional.**

WE HAVE TAKEN a brief tour of missions history, including God's ancient Old Testament waves of salvation, the Early Church Wave, the expansion of the church during the Middle Ages, and the three waves in modern missions to the coastlands, the interiors, and unreached peoples of the world.

A fourth wave of modern missions has begun that appears to be bigger than the rest. It needs to be. There are billions more people on earth than in earlier eras. The needs are greater, the opportunities are historic, and a broken world is waiting to hear about real hope and love that is found only in Jesus Christ.

I believe that the call of God in the fourth wave of modern missions is for *every believer on earth to be missional in the twenty-first century.* Led by millions of new believers from the Majority World nation, each one of us

can and should view ourselves as called to fulfill a mission—as a World
Christian who can

- pray passionately for a specific nation or nations;
- personally adopt an unreached people group for prayer and
  engagement;
- support churches and workers in the people group of our
  choosing;
- spend our vacations on mission in our city or country of adoption;
- live for years or a lifetime among a nation or people that God lays
  upon our heart.

If millions of Christians would personally adopt an unreached people
group, or commit to influence one of the four thousand Omega Zones
of Project 4K, then the completion of the Great Commission would be
greatly enhanced. This is the potential tsunami effect of the Fourth Wave:

*Every believer on earth taking their personal missions territory for the
advance of God's kingdom.*

We are the first generations in history to have the knowledge and
tools to reach every person in every nation of the world. In the past,

- Christians weren't fully aware of all the unreached masses in the
  world and didn't possess the technologies to reach everyone
  everywhere;
- a relatively small segment of the world population had the opportunity to be involved in Christ's global mission force;
- it was very difficult to travel to many nations and peoples around
  the world;
- the prevalence of disease killed many missionaries or stopped
  them from going;
- widespread poverty prevented many people from taking part in
  world evangelism;
- there were few places for women, youth, and children;
- missional roles were mostly limited to full-time professionals.

But in the Fourth Wave, very few of those restrictions will apply. Yes, in many nations, poverty and lack of opportunity will continue to be a challenge. It's also true that cross-cultural missionaries will still be needed to lead the charge of full engagement.

However, I believe that God will make a way for every believer to be missional. Because when you get right down to it—especially in our time when there are so many creative ways to participate in missions—it really boils down to having a missions heart.

Anyone with a missional passion will be empowered by God to catch the Fourth Wave.

Here are some stories to inspire you.[1]

Larry is a basketball player who struggled with his worth and identity on his native island of Puerto Rico. God got ahold of his life and allowed him to do short-term missionary work in the Philippines, where he met his wife, Richelle. Their young family is now working in another Asian nation where Larry is coaching and starting a professional Christian basketball team that can use sports to bring youth to Jesus. He has a vision for long-term sports ministry and involvement in business in that nation. *Larry is being missional.*

Nancy is an American senior citizen who struggled with depression. When God gave her a burden for the Roma people (Gypsies) in Europe, especially Romania, she began taking short-term trips to visit the people she was praying for, teach them some practical skills, and share her faith. Nancy now operates a website devoted to reaching and blessing the Roma. *Nancy is being missional.*

Bandhu and Pooja (not their real names) were born and raised in India and decided to move to Africa to teach young Muslim children and help improve their educational chances in life. They started a school in a poor village and are involved in a variety of evangelistic and humanitarian projects, primarily among an unreached Muslim people group. Their two children were raised in Africa. *Bandhu and Pooja are being missional.*

Chris is a computer geek and entrepreneur who wanted to use his skills to help in missions. Along with some other business partners, he formed a company that will soon be starting algae farms in Southeast Asia to produce biofuels and provide jobs for the local people. His heart is to use the company, its profits, and relationships formed through it to share Christ with the people of his newly adopted nation. *Chris is being missional.*

Enkhsuren was born into a poor family in Mongolia. As a young girl, she experienced abuse and the effects of alcoholism, and spent many nights outside in the frigid cold. She was known in her school as the "sad little girl." At the age of fourteen, she heard the gospel through a traveling children's performing arts team and gave her life to Christ. After earning her degree in Mongolia, she now serves as a cross-cultural missionary in the United States and has shared her faith in a number of countries. At twenty-six she has a vision for reaching native peoples and discipling her own nation. *Enkhsuren is being missional.*

Bill was in mid-life, his kids grown, and looking for the next thing to do. He'd always had a burden for government and politics, and had even written a book on the subject. After his daughter returned from a summer trip to Kosovo, a door opened for Bill to travel to that nation to teach a course on the Christian view of political science. He now has over one thousand students attending his courses at a leading university in that nation. *Bill is being missional.*

In the emerging fourth wave of modern missions, I believe large numbers of believers will join these and many others to adopt a people group for personalized focus, pray for them, support church planting and mission works among them, and use their talents and gifts in numerous missional ways to complete the Great Commission.

They will start in *their* Jerusalem (at home), but they will reach out to other Samarias and Judeas nearby (their state and nation). They will also have a heart for the "ends of the earth" because Jesus commanded them to make disciples of all nations.

They will pray, give, and go because others have gone before. They will be successful because the world is reachable and God will be with them. They will use all the tools a modern world has placed at their disposal. They could be the greatest or final generation in Christian missions.

This is no time to be ignorant about history and miss the wave. Grab your board (your gifts, talents, and passions), head for the beach (your neighborhood, across town, or around the world), and get up on that wave! It's heading toward the final shore.

"The Good News about the Kingdom will be preached throughout the whole world, so that all nations will hear it; and then the end will come" (Matt. 24:14).

The World Christians are coming. In the Fourth Wave everyone can be missional. Will you be one of them?

Part 4

A Spiritual Tsunami

"God has huge plans for the world today! He is not content to merely establish a handful of struggling churches among each tongue, tribe and nation. Even now He is preparing and empowering His Church to carry the seeds of revival to the uttermost ends of the earth."

—David Smithers

"'Not called!' did you say? 'Not heard the call,' I think you should say. Put your ear down to the Bible, and hear him bid you go and pull sinners out of the fire of sin. Put your ear down to the burdened, agonized heart of humanity, and listen to its pitiful wail for help. Go stand by the gates of hell, and hear the damned entreat you to go to their father's house and bid their brothers and sisters, and servants and masters not to come there. And then look Christ in the face, whose mercy you have professed to obey, and tell him whether you will join heart and soul and body and circumstances in the march to publish his mercy to the world."

—William Booth

Chapter 17

How Can I Catch the Wave?

HISTORY IS A HARD THING to accurately predict. World upheaval, recessions, and even deeper economic depressions could have a bearing on the forecasts made in this book. We also don't know exactly which nations and people will rise to the forefront of this emerging wave of missions. How much of it is dependent on human free will? What portion is set and determined by the sovereign plans of the Godhead?

What we do know is that the Fourth Wave of Modern Missions has already begun. New faces, races, nationalities, and methods are all being used to reach people for Christ. There is something powerfully holistic about this fresh wave of God's Spirit, as Sidle and Lewis explain:

> The old definition of mission as the Western church imperialistically sending missionaries to distant places is no longer viable. Missions is everything the local-global church is sent into the world to be and do as a participant in God's mission and every person and gift the local-global church receives in Christ's name and way. The missional practice of the local-global church must be holistic, with activities of evangelism, compassionate service, and social justice.[1]

The Missional Church

Each local church, in every nation of the world, must no longer think of missions as simply supporting workers overseas or going to another country. "Mission" or "missions" must become a *missional attitude* of using every means to reach every person everywhere. The local church must be missional in its neighborhood, missional in its state or nation, and missional in its global involvements. Missions outreach is not something we do—it is something we *are,* based on the commission of Jesus. Sidle and Lewis believe it is imperative that the church recognize its role as missionaries with God, through God, and by God's power. We must have "the mind of Christ" and be able to hear what God is saying to the church.[2]

Local churches in every nation must imbibe this missional attitude in every small group, Sunday school, corporate service, and training opportunity. Local churches must see themselves as living "cells" that must multiply their life both locally and globally. This fresh sense of global destiny should bring great growth and renewal to the churches of God in many nations around the world.

Refocus Education

Christian colleges, universities, and seminaries must also "reload" to take their place in the Fourth Wave. They should encourage their students to think globally and channel their talents for use in the growing kingdom of God in every sphere of life. Today's Christian students should learn to think as Christian *missionary* photographers, teachers, scientists, computer programmers, film makers, auto mechanics, homemakers, lawyers, doctors, parliamentarians, and every other trade and profession. They should be taught to fervently pray about *where* to use their skills for Christ in one of the 238 countries or among thousands of people groups in the world. They were born for this time of global missions.

Educators must motivate them to take their place. They should encourage their students to see their lives through a comprehensive Christian worldview as it relates to their life and vocation. They should sprinkle their coursework with modern missions stories of people who are using their talents for God to advance his kingdom. And they can pray and exhort their students to "go into all the world" to complete the Great Commission.

Pray for Global Revival

Because missional advance is predicated on fresh revivals of God's people, the power and efficacy of prayer, the importance of unity, and the use of modern technologies and godly strategies, every follower of Christ should seek to cooperate with God in all these vital arenas as never before. We should pray for a great global renewal of God's people. We should support and encourage growing movements of prayer. We should downplay any remaining denominational and organizational barriers and promote unity in the body of Christ for world evangelism. And we should encourage a Christian, missional, entrepreneurial spirit to be unleashed for the glory of God.

Pass the Torch

This is also a season in history for Western Christians to willingly pass the torch of world evangelization to their brothers and sisters in the Majority World. It doesn't mean that Westerners don't have a role to play—but rather that we recognize that a baton is being passed to Africans, Hispanics, Islanders, and Asians to take their place in God's sovereign plan. We will pray for them, support them, learn from them, and join them into the final harvest fields. We want China and India to be free to send forth millions of laborers. We desire Africans and Hispanics to circle the globe. This is their time—their moment of God-ordained opportunity. We must be their champions and grateful co-laborers.

Where Do I Begin?

There are a number of areas where every single believer can participate and fully support the fourth wave of modern missions:

Get informed about the unfinished task of world evangelization. A few of the comprehensive websites are:

- www.joshuaproject.net
- www.finishthetask.com
- www.call2all.org
- www.wycliffe.org
- www.imb.org
- www.operationworld.org
- www.uscwm.org

If you do not have Internet access, consider buying a copy of *Operation World* by Jason Mandryk.[3] I read it every day for years to educate myself about nations (or, for the larger countries, about their states or provinces) for regular intercession. Knowledge truly is power with God in the twenty-first century (Prov. 8:14).

Attend a Perspectives on the World Christian Movement course in your area.[4] Started by the U.S. Center for World Mission in 1974, this cutting-edge fifteen-week course on global missions has helped scores of thousands of believers to develop a passion for reaching those for whom Christ died.

Personally adopt an unreached people or nation. You may not be able to go long term to serve in that nation, but you can intercede fervently for its people and participate in its spiritual harvest by going on short-term trips or supporting others working there. This is the key to the Fourth Wave. Every Christian can be missional by choosing to focus their time, attention, and prayers on an unreached tribe, city, or nation in another part of the world. God will show you creative ways to engage in their evangelization.

Encourage your youth group, small group, or entire church to adopt and engage an unreached people. This step alone would breathe life and vitality into many churches worldwide. A number of years ago I encouraged a local congregation in our area to adopt an unreached people group in Africa. For the past ten years, that church has sent teams, workers, money, supplies, and has made a significant contribution to evangelism and church planting among their chosen people. Their commitment has revitalized their church and given them a focus outside of themselves. Every small group and youth group could experience the same if they adopted a people in another part of the world for whom they could especially pray and share the love of Christ.

Pray for China to become a free nation. This is one of the most strategic prayers you can pray in the twenty-first century. China is destined to be a vital nation in global evangelization, especially with its house church vision to take the gospel back to Jerusalem (the Back to Jerusalem movement). Micklethwait and Wooldridge say that if the democratization of China ever occurs, it could produce one of the greatest upticks in Christianity in world history.[5] They argue that democracy is about the people "finding their voice," and that the people of China "want to talk about God."[6] Pray fervently for liberty to come to every aspect of China and its vast population—and that God will use them to lead the Fourth Wave.

Pray for China and India to partner in global mission. These two most populous nations on earth have a key role to play in the dynamics of the twenty-first century. An alliance between the churches of both nations to send missionaries all over the world to preach the gospel would have a profound effect in our time.

Use your talent or vocation in missions. You've studied and prepared to be a businessperson, a teacher, a doctor or nurse, an engineer, carpenter, or computer programmer? Consider taking your skill to your adopted nation to use in meeting human needs and sharing the good news. Professional skills and business ventures open many doors for missionary service. In past eras, it was difficult for most to go. In today's world you are oftentimes only a visa and plane flight away from serving on the mission field.

Support local and international missions. Many of our urban cities are ripe for focused missional outreaches and activities of all types. In the Western world, serving in cities and various ethnic communities is a wonderful cross-cultural missions experience and opportunity. You can also set aside a portion of your income to devote to both local and international ministries that are meeting human needs and sharing the truth about Christ. Give generously! Your money follows your heart commitments (Matt. 6:21).

A Personal Story

As individuals, we must accept our calling as twenty-first century missionaries and throw our prayers and very lives into the people group or nation of God's choosing. I believe every Christian on earth should adopt at least one people group or nation as an object of their love and attention.

I've mentioned my "adoption" of the nation of Mongolia. To try and make a difference, I studied their history and culture. I started praying regularly for them, and I took a number of short-term trips to that nation. During my first five years of involvement, I recruited over one hundred other people to join me. We served in the countryside—where the people live in tent-like *gers*—and also in the capital city that houses half of Mongolia's population. We even sponsored a national youth conference to call Mongol youth into missions. It's been a challenging and exciting adventure.

When I first took on the burden for Mongolia, the church there was very small and the nation mired in extreme poverty. Today Mongolia has a developing economy and a church that has grown to fifty thousand. Mongolia had no known Christians in 1980. Today it is the number-one nation in the world for "Christians per sent missionary." It takes 222 Mongol Christians to send out one missionary. By comparison, the United States is thirtieth on the list of per capita sending nations—needing 2,148 senders for each missionary.[7]

The nation of Mongolia—never before involved in God's global plan—is taking its place in the Fourth Wave. Many other developing nations are doing the same.

I believe at the heart of the Fourth Wave, God desires hundreds of millions of twenty-first century Christians to adopt, engage, and share God's heart for a people group or nation on earth. I believe that for the first time in history, we will see people of all ages and nationalities taking the good news to every person on earth using innovative technologies and relational ministry in every sphere of society in every nation.

The sixteenth century Reformation restored the concept of the priesthood of all believers. The fourth wave of modern missions will restore the missional call of every Christian.

The final frontiers to reach with the good news are from the Pacific Rim, across Central and Western Asia, and back to Jerusalem. This final swath of kingdom expansion could just be the consummation stage of world missions.

If we rise to the challenge, the Fourth Wave just might be that sterling moment in history when the Great Commission is fulfilled and Jesus can return to set up his eternal kingdom (Matt. 24:14).

We might be the generation to bring back the King.

Whether this is the last great thrust in world evangelization, or the next significant move of missions advance, one thing remains the same. You have your assignment. The peoples of the earth are waiting. Now arise and go forth!

> Arise, Jerusalem! Let your light shine for all to see!
>> For the glory of the LORD rises to shine on you.
> Darkness as black as night covers all the nations of the earth,
>> but the glory of the LORD rises and appears over you.
> All nations will come to your light;
>> mighty kings will come to see your radiance. (Isa. 60:1–3)

Epilogue: A Word about Persecution and Suffering

This book focuses on the incredible move of God to advance the good news about Jesus all over the earth in the coming years. His work is ascendant, encouraging, and worthy of our time, attention, and prayers. Jesus is preparing a church to triumph—to finish the task of world evangelism. You may be a part of that magnificent plan.

But this does not mean that the task will be easy or without cost. Christian mission has always advanced during the darkest of eras— in fact, it is during the hardest of times that "the blood of the martyrs becomes the seed of the Church."[1]

Our era of destiny will be no different from the past. Though we are excited about the explosion in global missions that is before us in the Fourth Wave, we are well aware that our world may soon be entering difficult and chaotic times. The birth pangs could include

- increased global economic instability and uncertainty;
- a worldwide depression that could change our present way of life;
- increased warfare in the Middle East, or a Third World War;
- rising tensions between the ideologies of secularism, Islam, and the good news of Christ;
- increased famine and human need in the developing nations;
- the rise of totalitarian regimes—or even the long-promised one-world government that is spoken about in the Book of Revelation.

Only God knows what evils or judgments await us. They are within his providential guidance of history. But if history is any guide, then we can expect increased persecution and suffering during this period of triumph and advance. The two go hand in hand.

If you've never read *Foxe's Book of Martyrs*,[2] this might be a good time to purchase it and remind yourself that faith in Jesus conquers the powers of darkness through prayer, suffering, tribulation, and death. It has been so in every time period—from the Roman Christians who were thrown to the lions to the multitudes who suffered in the prison camps behind the Bamboo Curtain.[3]

In fact, the great explosion of Christian faith worldwide during the Third Wave of the twentieth century was accompanied by the greatest suffering and martyrdom in history. It is estimated that of the seventy million believers who were killed for their faith since the time of Christ, fully 65 percent of them perished in the twentieth century.[4]

In today's world, there is widespread persecution of Christians in the Molucca Islands of Indonesia, in Bangladesh, India, Nigeria, East Timor, Cuba, the former Soviet republics, Saudi Arabia and other Muslim countries, Vietnam, China, and others. As I was writing this chapter, ten Christian medical missionaries serving in Afghanistan were murdered by the Taliban. The reason? Taliban spokesman Zabiullah Mujahid told the press that they killed the foreigners because they were "spying for the Americans" and "preaching Christianity."[5]

If the Fourth Wave is destined to be greater than the Third, then possibly the greatest waves of persecution and death will also accompany this salvation harvest in the coming years.

But Jesus' comforting words remain the same in every generation:

Don't let your hearts be troubled. Trust in God, and trust also in me. There is more than enough room in my Father's home. . . . I am going to prepare a place for you. (John 14:1–2)

So don't be afraid, little flock. For it gives your Father great happiness to give you the Kingdom. (Luke 12:32)

The Father himself loves you dearly because you love me and believe that I came from God. Yes, I came from the Father into the world, and now I will leave the world and return to the Father. . . . The time is coming . . . when you will be scattered. . . . I have told you all this so that you may have peace in me. Here on earth you will have many trials and sorrows. But take heart, because I have overcome the world. (John 16:27, 32–33)

On a special shelf in my office sits one of the first Bibles given to me by my grandparents when I was a teenager. There is only one verse underlined in that Bible, and it means a great deal to me. Here are the dedicatory words underlined by my grandparents: "Be thou faithful unto death, and I will give thee a crown of life" (Rev. 2:10 KJV).

It's a great reminder.

Even though the wheat and the weeds will *both* voraciously grow during the time of the Fourth Wave and the End of the Age, there is no need to worry or shrink back.

Take your place in the swelling tide of missions and rest in his loving arms:

Can anything ever separate us from Christ's love? Does it mean he no longer loves us if we have trouble or calamity, or are persecuted, or hungry, or destitute, or in danger, or threatened with death? . . .

No, despite all these things, overwhelming victory is ours through Christ, who loved us.

And I am convinced that nothing can ever separate us from God's love. Neither death nor life, neither angels nor demons, neither our fears for today nor our worries about tomorrow—not even the powers of hell can separate us from God's love. No power in the sky above or in the earth below—indeed, nothing in all creation will ever be able to separate us from the love of God that is revealed in Christ Jesus our Lord. (Rom. 8:35, 37–39)

Appendix: Organizations and Online Resources

There are thousands of Christian missionary organizations in the world, and the number is growing. Some of the larger ones are listed below. A much broader list can be found in *Operation World* by Jason Mandryk, which can be ordered online at www.operationworld.org.

Missionary Organizations

Assemblies of God World Missions (www.worldmissions.ag.org)

Campus Crusade for Christ (www.campuscrusade.com)

Evangelical Missiological Society (www.emsweb.org)

Gospel for Asia (www.gfa.org)

Indian Evangelical Team (www.ietmissions.org)

International Fellowship of Evangelical Students (www.ifesworld.org)

Navigators (www.navigators.org/us)

New Tribes Mission (www.ntm.org)

Operation Mobilization (www.om.org)

OMF International (www.omf.org)

SBC–International Mission Board (www.imb.org)

SIM–Serving in Mission (www.sim.org)

U.S. Center for World Mission (www.uscwm.org)

WEC International (www.wec-int.org)

World Vision (www.worldvision.org)

Wycliffe Bible Translators (www.wycliffe.org)

Youth With A Mission (www.ywam.org)

Adopting an Unreached People Group

Call2All (www.call2all.org)

Finishing the Task (www.finishingthetask.com)

Joshua Project (www.joshuaproject.net)

Operation World (www.operationworld.org)

Global Mission Structures

Asia Missions Association (www.asiamissions.net)

COMIBAM International (Latin America) (www.comibam.org)

CrossGlobal Link (North America) (www.crossgloballink.org)

Evangelical Association of the Caribbean (www.caribbeanevangelical.org)

Global Network of Mission Structures (www.gnms.net)

Lausanne Movement (www.lausanne.org)

Movement of African National Initiatives (www.maniafrica.com)

World Evangelical Alliance (www.worldevangelicals.org)

Notes

Introduction

1. I will use the New Living Translation (NLT) for Scripture references unless noted otherwise.
2. Many major Protestant missionary organizations, such as the Southern Baptist Convention and the General Council of the Assemblies of God, use this term.
3. An example would be Roxburgh and Romanuk's *The Missional Leader: Equipping Your Church to Reach a Changing World* (San Francisco: Jossey-Bass, 2006).
4. Ralph Winter, "Four Men, Three Eras," *Mission Frontiers*, November/December 1997, 11.
5. Ibid., 12.
6. Ibid., 13.
7. Joshua Project, http://www.joshuaproject.net/.

Chapter 1

1. My book *Leadership for the 21st Century: Changing Nations Through the Power of Serving* was published the year the Iron Curtain came down. I had asked Lee Grady to help with chapter one, which contained a prophetic picture of communism's demise. Lee predicted the collapse in incredible detail, even the right order of the liberation of nations. He wrote his portion in 1986.
2. For more information visit http://www.ywam.org/.
3. For a full discussion of Korea's history and missionary beginnings, see Djun Kil Kim's *The History of Korea* (Westport, Conn.: Greenwood Press, 2005).
4. Andrei Lankov, "North Korea's Missionary Position," *Asian Times*, March 16, 2005.
5. Yoido Full Gospel Church, http://www.ambassador4christ.org/yoido_church .html.
6. A good article on the amazing Tanghwajin Missionary Cemetery can be found at http://trifter.com/asia-pacific/seoul-foreigners-cemetery-a-quiet -stroll-through-history/.
7. This story is well chronicled in Gavin Menzie's fascinating book *1421: The Year China Discovered America* (New York: HarperCollins, 2003).

8. John Micklethwait and Adrian Wooldridge, *God Is Back: How the Global Revival of Faith is Changing the World* (New York: Penguin Press, 2009), 5.

9. Christian Zibreg, "China Is Now the World's Second-Largest Economy, Will Pass the U.S. by 2025," http://www.geek.com/articles/news/china-is-now-the -worlds-second-largest-economy-will-pas-the-us-by-2025-2010082/.

10. See Rodney Stark, "The Sin of Slavery," in *For the Glory of God: How Monotheism Led to Reformations, Science, Witch-Hunts, and the End of Slavery* (Princeton, N.J.: Princeton University Press, 2003), 291–366.

11. Todd Johnson, *The Atlas of Global Christianity 1910–2010* (Edinburgh: Edinburgh University Press, 2009), 311.

12. Ibid., 310.

13. You can read the story of the Global Day of Prayer and its many initiatives at http://www.globaldayofprayer.com/.

14. Mosab Hassan Yousef's story is told in *Son of Hamas: A Gripping Account of Terror, Betrayal, Political Intrigue, and Unthinkable Choice* (Carol Stream, Ill.: SaltRiver, 2010).

15. Sarah Stegall, "Evangelists Say Muslims Coming to Christ at Historic Rate," *Charisma News Online,* August 20, 2010, http://www.charismamag.com/index .php/news/29125-evangelists-say-muslims-coming-to-christ-at-historic-rate.

16. "Dreams and Visions of Jesus," The 30-Days Prayer Network, http://www.30 -days.net/muslims/muslims-in/mid-near-east/dreams-visions/.

17. Patrick Johnstone and Jason Mandryk, *Operation World,* 6th ed. (Bromley, UK: Send the Light Publishing, 2007), 311.

18. This is Gene Edwards's conclusion in his classic book *A Tale of Three Kings: A Study in Brokenness* (Wheaton, Ill.: Tyndale House, 1992).

Chapter 2

1. Loren Cunningham, *Is That Really You, God?* (Grand Rapids: Chosen Books, 1984), 30.

2. See Loren Cunningham, *The Book That Transforms Nations: The Power of the Bible to Change Any Country* (Seattle: YWAM Publishing, 2007).

Chapter 3

1. Leslie T. Lyall, *A World to Win* (London: InterVarsity Press, 1972), 6.

2. Loren Cunningham, *Is That Really You, God?* (Grand Rapids: Chosen Books, 1984), 30.

3. J. Herbert Kane, *Christian Missions in Biblical Perspective* (Grand Rapids: Baker Book House, 1976), 98.

4. Kenneth Scott Latourette, *A History of Christianity* (Peabody, Mass.: Prince Press, 2000), 59.

5. Dennis and Rita Bennett, *The Holy Spirit and You: A Study Guide to the Spirit-Filled Life* (Plainfield, N.J.: Logos International, 1971), 27–29.

6. Ibid., 29. Father Bennett was the rector at St. Luke's Episcopal Church in Seattle for many years and authored many books and spoke all over the world about the renewal of the Holy Spirit in the sixties and seventies. His first book, entitled

Nine O'Clock in the Morning, was the flagship treatise of the charismatic renewal in its early years.

7. E. Glenn Hinson, *The Evangelization of the Roman Empire: Identity and Adaptability* (Macon, Ga.: Mercer University Press, 1981), 57.

8. Ibid., 58.

9. Harold R. Cook, *Highlights of Christian Missions* (Chicago: Moody Press, 1967), 16.

10. Michael Pocock, Gailyn Van Rheenen, and Douglas McConnell, *The Changing Face of Missions: Engaging Contemporary Issues and Trends* (Grand Rapids: Baker Academic, 2005), 49.

11. Rodney Stark, *Discovering God* (New York: Harper Collins, 2007), 310.

12. Ibid., 313. Stark's "Christian Growth Chart" projects that the early church began with about one thousand believers in AD 40 but had reached over thirty-one million followers of Christ by AD 350, representing nearly 53 percent of the Roman world.

13. Kane, *Christian Missions in Biblical Perspective,* 258.

14. One of my favorite books on this period is Thomas Cahill's modern classic *How the Irish Saved Civilization* (New York: Doubleday, 1995). Without the literary skills of the courageous monk-missionaries of the Middle Ages, not only the Bible but also many of the great writings of Western civilization might have been lost to antiquity.

Chapter 4

1. Moon Tides, http://home.hiwaay.net/~krcool/Astro/moon/moontides/.

2. I gave my life to Christ in 1968 during a period of renewal known as the Jesus Revolution. I have seen God move in revival power in both Africa and the United States. I met my wife in a youth revival in our hometown that touched 150 young people in 1974–75 and launched many into missions. I was the capital city coordinator for the Washington for Jesus rally on April 29, 1980, that brought 700,000 Americans to Washington, DC, to pray for spiritual revival. Six months later, Ronald Reagan was elected president of the United States on the theme of "Morning in America"—a very apt description of the need for spiritual renewal in our nation.

3. The preceding definitions are taken from *An Urgent Appeal: To Christian Leaders in America for Consensus and Collaboration on the Biblical Nature and Hope of Corporate Revival* (Westminister, Colo.: National Revival Network, 2001).

4. Charles Finney, *Revival Lectures* (Grand Rapids: Fleming Revell, 1993), 7.

5. The ten-day reference is the time frame between Jesus' ascension on the fortieth day after his resurrection and the coming of the Holy Spirit on Pentecost, the fiftieth day.

6. Ralph Winter, "The Finishable Task!" *Mission Frontiers,* March 1989, 14.

7. Thomas Cahill, *How the Irish Saved Civilization: The Untold Story of Ireland's Heroic Role from the Fall of Rome to the Rise of Medieval Europe* (New York: Doubleday, 1995).

8. Winter, "The Finishable Task!" 15.

9. A good resource on the Moravians is "A Short Introduction to the History, Customs, and Practices of the Moravian Church" by Herbert Spaugh, http://every daycounselor.net/?p=105.

10. Robert Tuttle, *John Wesley: His Life and Theology* (Grand Rapids: Zondervan, 1978), 181–192.

11. Robert K. Greenleaf, *Servant Leadership: A Journey into the Nature of Legitimate Power and Greatness* (New York: Paulist Press, 1977), 62–66.

12. Quoted by Verna M. Hall, *The Christian History of the Constitution of the United States of America* (San Francisco: Foundation for American Christian Education, 1966), Ia.

13. Arnold Guyot, *Physical Geography* (Princeton, N.J.: Princeton Press, 1873), 5.

14. Todd Johnson, *The Atlas of Global Christianity 1910–2010* (Edinburgh: Edinburgh University Press, 2009), 310.

15. University of Texas professor Rodney Stark devotes one chapter of his book *For the Glory of God* to the connection between biblical faith and the rise of modern science. Stark includes a list of over one hundred of the world's first scientists who believed in a Creator God who made an orderly world for man to understand and develop.

Chapter 5

1. Ruth Tucker, *From Jerusalem to Irian Jaya: A Biographical History of Christian Missions* (Grand Rapids: Zondervan, 1983), 91.

2. Bruce L. Shelley, *Church History in Plain Language* (Waco, Tex.: Word, 1982), 274–275.

3. Tucker, *From Jerusalem to Irian Jaya*, 100.

4. Kenneth Scott Latourette, *A History of Christianity, Volume 2: A.D. 1500–A.D. 1975* (New York: Harper & Row, 1975), 961.

5. Tucker, *From Jerusalem to Irian Jaya*, 102.

6. Ibid., 121.

7. Ibid.

8. Ibid., 123.

9. William Carey, *An Enquiry into the Obligations of Christians to Use Means for the Conversion of the Heathens* (Leicester, England: Ann Richards printer, 1792), 37.

10. Ibid., 62.

11. Ibid., 87.

12. Latourette, *A History of Christianity, Volume 2*, 961. Latourette's term "the Great Century" of missions refers to the time period 1815–1914 and includes primarily Protestant outreach during the period.

13. Tucker, *From Jerusalem to Irian Jaya*, 126.

14. Ibid., 130.

15. Shelley, *Church History in Plain Language*, 374.

16. Edward B. Cole, *The Baptist Heritage* (Elgin, Ill.: David C. Cook, 1976), 47–52.

17. Latourette, *A History of Christianity, Volume 2*, 1047–55.

18. John Wesley, *The Journal of John Wesley* (Chicago: Moody Press, 1972), 56.

19. Ibid., 419.

20. R. C. Sproul and Archie Parrish, *The Spirit of Revival: Discovering the Wisdom of Jonathan Edwards* (Wheaton, Ill.: Crossway Books, 2000), 22–24.

21. *America's Great Revivals* (Minneapolis: Bethany Fellowship, 1976), 12.

22. J. Edwin Orr, *The Eager Feet* (Chicago: Moody Press, 1975), 89.

23. Courtney Anderson, *To the Golden Shore: The Life of Adoniram Judson* (Valley Forge, Pa.: Judson, 1987), 42.

24. According to Thomas Cahill, much of the record of the missionary advance of the early centuries perished during the upheaval of the Middle Ages associated with the sack of Rome and fall of the Roman Empire.

25. A. E. Medlycott, *India and the Apostle Thomas* (London: Cambridge Publishers, 1905), 221–225.

26. Thomas Cahill, *How the Irish Saved Civilization: The Untold Story of Ireland's Heroic Role from the Fall of Rome to the Rise of Medieval Europe* (New York: Doubleday, 1995), 107.

27. Ibid., 206.

28. Paul Gray, "Johann Gutenberg (c. 1395–1468)," *Time,* December 26, 1999, 23.

29. David M. Howard, ed., *Jesus Christ: Lord of the Universe, Hope of the World* (Downers Grove, Ill.: InterVarsity Press, 1974), 115.

30. Gavin Menzies, *1421: The Year China Discovered America* (New York: Perennial, 2004), chronicles the legendary voyages of the Ming Dynasty's Zheng He and his famous floating armada.

31. Howard, *Jesus Christ,* 115.

Chapter 6

1. This phrase describing the mystery of the unexplored portions of Africa was popularized by Henry M. Stanley in his 1878 publication *Through the Dark Continent.* Stanley was the journalist who tracked down David Livingstone in Africa and greeted him with the famous words, "Dr. Livingstone, I presume."

2. J. H. Worcester, Jr., *David Livingstone: First to Cross Africa with the Gospel* (Chicago: Moody Press, 1988), 14–16.

3. Ibid., 17.

4. Ibid., 85.

5. Ibid., 46.

6. Ibid., 110.

7. Ibid.

8. Carl Lawrence and David Wang, *The Coming Influence of China* (Gresham, Ore.: Vision House, 1996), 3.

9. Fred Barlow, *Profiles in Evangelism: Biographical Sketches of World-Renowned Soul Winners* (Murphreesboro, Tenn.: Sword of the Lord, 1976), 2.

10. J. C. Pollock, *Hudson Taylor and Maria: Pioneers in China* (Grand Rapids: Zondervan, 1976), 45.

11. Ibid., 49–50.

12. Marshall Broomhall, ed., *Martyred Missionaries of the China Inland Mission* (London: Morgan & Scott, 1901), 334.

13. Ibid.

14. Ibid.

15. Pollock, *Hudson Taylor and Maria*, 208.

16. Barlow, *Profiles in Evangelism*, 3.

17. Pollock, *Hudson Taylor and Maria*, 267.

18. Ralph D. Winter and Steven C. Hawthorne, eds., *Perspectives on the World Christian Movement: A Reader* (Pasadena: William Carey Library, 1981).

19. John R. Mott, *Cooperation and the World Mission* (London: Student Christian Movement Press, 1935), 87.

20. Ibid., 88.

21. Ruth Tucker, *From Jerusalem to Irian Jaya: A Biographical History of Christian Missions* (Grand Rapids: Zondervan, 1983), 324.

22. J. Edwin Orr, *The Eager Feet: Evangelical Awakenings, 1790–1830* (Chicago: Moody Press, 1975), 196.

23. *America's Great Revivals*, (Minneapolis: Bethany Fellowship, 1976), 78–82.

24. Ron Boehme, "Prayer Is the Gunpowder of Missions," YWAM Office of U.S. Renewal, http://usrenewal.squarespace.com/home/2010/1/29/prayer-is-the -gunpowder-of-global-missions.html. The article was originally published in the book *Giving Ourselves to Prayer* by Dan R. Crawford (Terre Haute, Ind.: Prayer Shop Publishing, 2008).

25. *America's Great Revivals*, 52–72.

26. Tucker, *From Jerusalem to Irian Jaya*, 324.

27. Kenneth Scott Latourette, *A History of Christianity, Volume 2: A.D. 1500–A.D. 1975* (New York: Harper & Row, 1975), 1325.

28. David M. Howard, *Jesus Christ: Lord of the Universe, Hope of the World* (Downers Grove, Ill.: InterVarsity Press, 1974), 127.

29. Latourette, *A History of Christianity, Volume 2*, 1068–69.

30. Ibid., 4.

31. Tucker, *From Jerusalem to Irian Jaya*, 285.

Chapter 7

1. Ruth A. Tucker, *From Jerusalem to Irian Jaya: A Biographical History of Christian Missions* (Grand Rapids: Zondervan, 1983), 364.

2. As chronicled in the groundbreaking atlas of global Christianity by David B. Barrett, ed., *World Christian Encyclopedia: A Comparative Study of Churches and Religions in the Modern World, AD 1900–2000* (New York: Oxford University Press, 1982), 3.

3. Patrick Johnstone, *The Church Is Bigger Than You Think* (Pasadena: William Carey Library, 1998), 218.

4. Wheaton Archives, http://www.wheaton.edu/bgc/archives/guides/178.htm#301.

5. Ralph D. Winter and Steven C. Hawthorne, eds., *Perspectives on the World Christian Movement: A Reader* (Pasadena: William Carey Library, 1981), 137.

6. Claude Hickman, "William Cameron Townsend," available at The Traveling Team, http://www.thetravelingteam.org/node/125.

7. "The Greatest Missionary," *Houston Baptist University* 3, no. 2 (January–March 2006): 3.

8. Wycliffe Bible Translators, http://www.wycliffe.org/About/Statistics.aspx.

9. Claude Hickman, "William Cameron Townsend," http://www.thetraveling team.org/node/125.

10. "U.S. Center for World Mission Celebrating 25 Years of Service," U.S. Center for World Mission.

11. U.S. Center for World Mission, "Our Vision and Mission," http://www.uscwm .org/index.php/about/.

12. Ralph D. Winter, "What Is an Unreached People Group?" *Mission Frontiers,* May/June 1995, 1.

13. The 10/40 Window refers to those regions of the Eastern Hemisphere located between 10 and 40 degrees north of the equator. The 10/40 Window concept highlights these three elements: countries in an area of the world with (1) great poverty, (2) low quality of life, and (3) least access to Christian resources. The Window forms a band encompassing Saharan and Northern Africa, as well as almost all of Asia (West Asia, Central Asia, South Asia, East Asia, and much of Southeast Asia). Roughly two-thirds of the world population lives in the 10/40 Window. The 10/40 Window is populated by people who are predominantly Muslim, Hindu, Buddhist, Animist, Jewish, or atheist. Many governments in the 10/40 Window are formally or informally opposed to Christian work of any kind.

14. Luis Bush, *Funding World Missions* (Wheaton, Ill.: World Evangelical Fellowship Missions Commission, 1990), 9.

15. Yoido Full Gospel Church, "Story," http://english.fgtv.com/yfgc.pdf.

16. Robert Moll, "Mission Incredible," *Christianity Today,* March 2006, 3.

17. Ibid., 4.

18. Gospel for Asia, http://www.gfa.org/about/aboutkp/.

19. K. P. Yohannan, *Revolution in World Missions* (Carrolton, Tex.: Gospel for Asia Books, 2000), 18.

20. Brother Yun, *The Heavenly Man* (Grand Rapids: Kregel Publications, 2002), 25.

21. Ibid., 107–131.

22. Ibid., 279.

23. Ibid., 289.

24. The Embassy of the Blessed Kingdom of All Nations, http://www.family aidinternational.com/embassy_of_god/who_is_sunday_adelaja.htm.

25. Philip Jenkins, *The New Faces of Christianity: Believing the Bible in the Global South* (New York: Oxford University Press, 2006), 47.

26. Todd Johnson and Kenneth R. Ross, eds., *The Atlas of Global Christianity 1910–2010* (Edinburgh: Edinburgh University Press, 2009), 311.

27. Johnstone, *The Church Is Bigger Than You Think,* 129.

28. Carl Lawrence and David Wang, *The Coming Influence of China* (Gresham, Ore.: Vision House, 1996), 85.

29. David Aikman, *Jesus in Beijing: How Christianity Is Transforming China and Changing the Global Balance of Power* (Washington, DC: Regnery Press, 2006), 47.

30. Bush, *Funding World Missions,* 480.

31. Grant Wacker, *The Functions of Faith in Primitive Pentecostalism* (New York: Cambridge University Press, 1984), 353.

32. Luis Lugo, "The Pentecostal Revival," *Ministry Today*, March 2, 2010, 22.

33. Scott Moreau, as quoted by Rob Moll, "Missions Incredible," *Christianity Today*, March 2006, 36.

34. Johnstone, *The Church Is Bigger Than You Think*, 34–40.

Chapter 8

1. Charles Clarke, *Pioneers of Revival* (Plainfield, N.J.: Logos International, 1971), 28.

2. Ibid., 28.

3. Ibid., 30.

4. J. Edwin Orr, *The Re-Study of Revival and Revivalism* (Oxford: Oxford Press, 1981), 43.

5. Vinson Synan, *The Holiness-Pentecostal Tradition: Charismatic Movements in the Twentieth Century* (Grand Rapids: Eerdmans, 1997), 130.

6. Clarke, *Pioneers of Revival*, 39–42.

7. I personally sat under the teaching of one of the leaders of the Congo Revival, New Zealander Ivor Davies, who shared these stories with his students in a series of meetings in 1972.

8. Mathew Backholer, *150 Years of Revival*, http://www.byfaith.co.uk/paulbyfaithtvmathewthoughts18.htm.

9. Andrew Woolsey, *Duncan Campbell: A Biography* (London: Hodder & Stoughton, 1974), 112–120.

10. The author gave his life to Christ in the middle of the Jesus Revolution and charismatic renewal in the spring of 1968.

11. Mel Tari, *Like A Mighty Wind* (Houston: New Leaf, 1995), 150–178.

12. "A. T. Pierson Quotes," http://christian-quotes.ochristian.com/A.T.-Pierson-Quotes/.

13. I was once visiting Seoul, Korea, and was told by my host, a Presbyterian pastor, that his church was involved in forty days of prayer and fasting. I asked him if they did this once a year. He replied, "No, we do it four times a year." I was amazed at the prayer commitment of the Korean believers.

14. Peggy Noonan, "We Want God," http://usrenewal.squarespace.com/home/2009/2/13/we-want-god.html.

15. 24/7 Prayer, http://www.24-7prayer.com.

16. See You at the Pole, www.syatp.com.

17. International Renewal Ministries, http://www.prayersummits.net.

18. The Global Day of Prayer, http://www.globaldayofprayer.com.

19. George W. Peters, "Missionary Dynamic and Prayer," in *Giving Ourselves to Prayer*, ed. Dan R. Crawford (Terre Haute, Ind.: Prayer Shop Publishing, 2008), 541.

20. Cape Town 2010, http://www.lausanne.org/cape-town-2010.

21. AD2000 and Beyond, http://www.ad2000.org/.

22. Luis Bush, "The Unfinished Task," *Mission Frontiers* May/June 1998, 28.

23. Call2All, http://www.call2all.org/Groups/1000015933/Call2All/About_Us /Dr_Bill_Bright/Dr_Bill_Bright.aspx.

24. King's Kids International, http://www.kkint.net.

25. Rob Moll, "Missions Incredible," *Christianity Today*, March 2006, 36.

26. Brother Yun, *The Heavenly Man* (Grand Rapids: Kregel Publications, 2002), 278–292.

27. Michael Pocock, Gail Van Rheenen, and Douglas McConnell, *The Changing Face of Missions: Engaging Contemporary Issues and Trends* (Grand Rapids: Baker Academic, 2005), 134.

28. Roger Peterson, "What's Happening in Short-Term Mission?" *Lausanne World Pulse*, March 2010, 2.

29. Warren Janzen, "The Springboard of Short-Term Missions," *Lausanne World Pulse*, March 2010, 2.

30. Ruth Tucker, *From Jerusalem to Irian Jaya: A Biographical History of Christian Missions* (Grand Rapids: Zondervan, 1983), 111.

31. A. Hinman, "Eradication of Vaccine-Preventable Diseases," *Annual Review of Public Health* 20 (May 1999), available at http://arjournals.annualreviews.org /doi/abs/10.1146%2Fannurev.publhealth.20.1.211.

32. The "JESUS" film, a ministry of Campus Crusade for Christ, http://www .jesusfilm.org/.

33. I have worked extensively in Mongolia since 1997 and have heard this analysis from many of the pastors in that nation.

34. John Dawson, *Taking Our Cities for God: How to Break Spiritual Strongholds* (Lake Mary, Fla.: Creation House, 1989), 63.

Chapter 9

1. Quoted in Rick Wood, "Christianity: Waning or Growing?" *Mission Frontiers*, January/February 2003, 12.

2. William Carey, *An Enquiry in the Obligation of Christians to Use means for the Conversion of the Heathens*, (Leicester, England: Ann Richards printer, 1792), 38–61.

3. Todd Johnson, "Status of Global Missions," Center for the Study of Global Christianity (www.globalchristianity.org).

4. "Unengaged Unreached People Groups (UUPGs)," http://www.call2all.org /Groups/1000014484/Call2All/About_Us/Themes/UUPGs/UUPGs.aspx.

5. Rick Warren, "The Future of Evangelicalism," *Pew Forum Newsletter*, November 20, 2009, 3.

6. Todd Johnson, "World Missions Statistics," Center for the Study of Global Christianity (www.globalchristianity.org).

7. "YWAM International Statistics," Youth With A Mission, http://old.ywam.org /notfound.asp?404;http%3A//old.ywam.org%3A80/contents/sta_res_stats .htm&bhcp=1.

8. David Taylor, "Envisioning a Global Network of Mission Structures," *Mission Frontiers*, March/April 2010, 16.

Chapter 10

1. Jim Stier, "The Fourth Wave," *The Flame Goes Forward* (National City, Calif.: YWAM San Diego/Baja), 160. Jim's list includes all generations, international, globalized, orality and viral communication, in all the spheres of life, world-oriented, marked by power and unity, and Kingdom focused.
2. King's Kids International, http://www.kkint.net/index.php?id=8.

Chapter 11

1. David Taylor, "Setting the Pace," *Mission Frontiers,* July/August 2010, 6.
2. Ibid., 7.
3. One example is Olu Robbin-Coker, originally from Sierra Leone and author of *Manifesto: Revolutionary Christianity for a Postmodern World*, who is making a difference in the nation of Scotland.
4. Handbook of Hispanic Protestant Denominations, http://www.hispanic churchesusa.net/.
5. Peter Hammond, "Muslims Coming to Christ," Frontline Fellowship, http://www.frontline.org.za/articles/Muslims%20coming%20to%20Christ.htm.
6. See Garrison's excellent website at http://www.churchplantingmovements.com.
7. David Garrison, *Church Planting Movements: How God Is Redeeming a Lost World* (Midlothian, Tex.: WIGTake Resources, 2004), 32–50.

Chapter 12

1. William Carey, *An Enquiry into the Obligations of Christians to Use Means for the Conversion of the Heathens* (Leicester, England: Ann Richards printer, 1792), 62.
2. *World Population to 2300* (New York: United Nations, 2004), 27.
3. Ibid.
4. David Taylor, "Setting the Pace," *Mission Frontiers,* July/August 2010, 5.
5. Call2All, http://www.call2all.org/Groups/1000014360/Call2All.aspx.
6. http://www.4kworldmap.com/.

Chapter 13

1. http://www.febc.org/about/history.html.
2. Trans World Radio, "The Future is Here," http://www.twr.org/pdfs/Futureis Herebooklet09.pdf.
3. Ibid.
4. "Media Statistics: Televisions (most recent) by country," http://www.nation master.com/graph/med_tel-media-televisions.
5. CBN: The Christian Broadcasting Network, http://www.cbn.com/.
6. TBN: Trinity Broadcasting Network, http://www.tbn.org/.
7. Shiryawati's story can be found at http://www.god.tv/node/118.
8. http://www.jesusfilm.org/.
9. Create International, http://www.createinternational.com/.
10. Joshua Newton, "Blockbuster Evangelism," *Christianity Today,* December 2003, http://www.christianitytoday.com/ct/2003/december/12.28.html.

11. Ibid.

12. Paul Eshleman, "The State of the Unifinished Task," *Mission Frontiers*, July/August 2010, 1.

13. Orality Strategies, http://www.oralstrategies.com/index.cfm.

14. "Cattlemen Connect in Southern Sudan," Orality Strategies, http://www.oral strategies.com/stories_detail.cfm?ResourceID=754.

15. "Mobile Phones and Other Devices: The Potential for Evangelism," Internet Evangelism Day, http://www.internetevangelismday.com/mobile-outreach.php.

16. http://tinyurl.com/pewinternet-mobiles.

17. Electa Draper, "Bible Translators Hope to Have Every Language Covered in Fifteen Years," *Denver Post*, June 22, 2010.

18. Global Media Outreach, http://www.globalmediaoutreach.com/about_us.html.

19. Ibid.

20. "Tokyo 2010's New Technology Vision," *Mission Frontiers*, July/August 2010, 24.

21. "Tokyo 2010 Declaration," *Mission Frontiers*, July/August 2010, 14.

Chapter 14

1. http://www.web-evangelism.com/resources/webull06mar1.php#shy_girl_-_a_blogger_s_story

2. http://www.whybelieve.com/.

3. Nathalie's site can be found at http://knowinggod.jesus.net.

4. The Center for Bio-Ethical Reform lists estimates from the Guttmacher Institute showing that there are approximately 42 million abortions a year worldwide (1996–2008), http://www.abortionno.org/Resources/fastfacts.html.

Chapter 15

1. Miss Hall and Miss Slater started the Foundation for American Christian Education (FACE), a major contributor to research and training on the "Principle-Approach" in America's Christian history.

2. Ron Boehme, *Leadership for the 21st Century: Changing Nations Through the Power of Serving* (Seattle: YWAM Publishing, 1989), 10.

3. Rodney Stark's excellent work *For the Glory of God: How Monotheism Led to Reformations, Science, Witch-Hunts, and the End of Slavery* (Princeton, N.J.: Princeton University Press, 2003) chronicles many of these aspects of Christian cultural development.

4. John Micklethwait and Adrian Wooldridge, *God Is Back: How the Global Revival of Faith Is Changing the World* (New York: Penguin Press, 2009), 12.

5. Tom Bloomer, "Calvin and Geneva: Nation-Building Mission," in *His Kingdom Come: An Integrated Approach to Discipling the Nations and Fulfilling the Great Commission,* eds. Jim Stier, Richlyn Poor, and Lisa Orvis (Seattle: YWAM Publishing, 2008), 103–118.

6. Loren Cunningham, *The Book That Transforms Nations: The Power of the Bible to Change Any Country* (Seattle: YWAM Publishing, 2007).

7. Matthew Henry, "Commentary on Matthew 28[:19]," Blue Letter Bible, 1996,

    2011, http://www.blueletterbible.org/commentaries/comm_view.cfm?Author
ID=4&contentID=1623&commInfo=5&topic=Matthew.

8. *Discipling Nations* (2001) and *LifeWork* (2009) are both published by YWAM Publishing.

9. In *Truth and Transformation: A Manifesto for Ailing Nations* (Seattle: YWAM Publishing, 2009), Mangalwadi shares many personal stories of hope and transformation through Christ.

10. *His Kingdom Come,* eds. Jim Stier, Richlyn Poor, and Lisa Orvis (Seattle: YWAM Publishing, 2008) includes chapters by twenty-nine authors.

11. See http://www.dawnministries.org and http://call2all.org, respectively.

12. Micklethwait and Wooldridge, *God Is Back,* 355.

13. Story taken from my own work, *Leadership for the 21st Century: Changing Nations Through the Power of Serving* (Seattle: YWAM Publishing, 1989), 117.

14. Herman Dooyeweerd, *Roots of Western Culture: Pagan, Secular, and Christian Options* (Toronto: Wedge, 1979), 53.

15. Abraham Kuyper, *Lectures on Calvinism* (Grand Rapids: Eerdmans, 1931, 1975), 3.

16. Ibid., 6.

17. Story is found in Landa Cope's chapter, "The Old Testament Template for Discipling Nations," in *His Kingdom Come,* eds. Jim Stier, Richlyn Poor, and Lisa Orvis (Seattle: YWAM Publishing, 2008), 31–44.

18. Taken from http://www.templateinstitute.com/.

Chapter 16

1. These examples are true stories of personal friends of mine.

Chapter 17

1. Patricia Lloyd-Sidle and Bonnie Sue Lewis, *Teaching Mission in a Global Context* (Louisville, Ky.: Geneva Press, 2001), 52.

2. Ibid., 125.

3. Jason Mandryk, *Operation World,* 7th ed., (Colorado Springs: Biblica, 2010). Some of the information from the book is available at http://www.operation world.org/.

4. Perspectives on the World Christian Movement, http://www.perspectives.org/. For classes and curriculum outside the United States, go to the "Around the World" page.

5. John Micklethwait and Adrian Wooldridge, *God Is Back* (New York: Penguin Press, 2009), 355.

6. For more information on the Back to Jerusalem movement, see Brother Yun's *The Heavenly Man* (Grand Rapids: Kregel Publications, 2002), which tells the story of the Chinese house church revival, and especially chapter 24, "Back to Jerusalem," on pages 278–292.

7. Multi-media presentation, September 2010, by Bob Waymire, President, LIGHT International.

Epilogue

1. This is an oft-quoted paraphrase from chapter 50 of *Apologeticus* by the second-century church father Tertullian.
2. This classic book by John Foxe, though originally published in 1573, has been updated to include the present era. John Foxe and Harold J. Chadwick, *The New Foxe's Book of Martyrs* (Gainesville, Fla.: Bridge Logos, 2001).
3. Ibid., 329.
4. Chuck Colson, "A New Century of Martyrs: Anti-Christian Intolerance," June 17, 2002, http://www.bereanpublishers.com/Persecution_of_Christians/a_new_century_of_martyrs.htm.
5. Kathy Gannon, "Six Americans on Medical Team Killed in Afghanistan," August 7, 2010, http://www.ksdk.com/news/local/story.aspx?storyid=210884.

Bibliography

Aikman, David. *Jesus in Beijing: How Christianity Is Transforming China and Changing the Global Balance of Power.* Washington, DC: Regnery Press, 2003.

Anderson, Courtney. *To the Golden Shore: The Life of Adoniram Judson.* Valley Forge, Pa.: Judson Press, 1987.

America's Great Revivals. Minneapolis: Bethany Fellowship, 1976.

Barlow, Fred. *Profiles in Evangelism: Biographical Sketches of World-Renowned Soul Winners.* Murfreesboro, Tenn.: Sword of the Lord, 1976.

Barrett, David B. *World Christian Encyclopedia: A Comparative Study of Churches and Religions in the Modern World, AD 1900–2000.* New York: Oxford University Press, 1982.

Bennett, Dennis, and Rita Bennett. *The Holy Spirit and You: A Study Guide to the Spirit-Filled Life.* Plainfield, N.J.: Logos International, 1971.

Boehme, Ron. *Leadership for the 21st Century: Changing Nations Through the Power of Serving.* Seattle: YWAM Publishing, 1989.

Bush, Luis. *Funding World Missions.* Wheaton, Ill.: World Evangelical Fellowship Missions Commission, 1990.

Cahill, Thomas. *How the Irish Saved Civilization: The Untold Story of Ireland's Heroic Role from the Fall of Rome to the Rise of Medieval Europe.* New York: Doubleday, 1995.

Carey, William. *An Enquiry in the Obligation of Christians to Use Means for the Conversion of the Heathens.* Leicester, England: Ann Richards printer, 1792.

Cheever, George B. *The Journal of the Pilgrims at Plymouth.* New York: J. Wiley, 1848.

Clarke, Charles. *Pioneers of Revival.* Plainfield, N.J.: Logos International, 1971.

Cole, Edward B. *The Baptist Heritage.* Elgin, Ill.: David C. Cook, 1976.

Cook, Harold R. *Highlights of Christian Missions: A History and Survey.* Chicago: Moody Press, 1967.

Crawford, Dan R. *Giving Ourselves to Prayer.* Terre Haute, Ind.: Prayer Shop Publishing, 2008.

Cunningham, Loren. *Is That Really You, God?* Grand Rapids: Chosen Books, 1984.

————. *The Book That Transforms Nations: The Power of the Bible to Change Any Country.* Seattle: YWAM Publishing, 2007.

Dawson, John. *Taking Our Cities for God: How to Break Spiritual Strongholds.* Lake Mary, Fla.: Creation House, 1989.

Dooyeweerd, Herman. *Roots of Western Culture: Pagan, Secular, and Christian Options.* Toronto: Wedge, 1979.

Edwards, Gene. *A Tale of Three Kings: A Study in Brokenness.* Wheaton, Ill.: Tyndale House, 1992.

Finney, Charles. *Revival Lectures.* Grand Rapids: Fleming Revell, 1993.

Garrison, David. *Church Planting Movements: How God Is Redeeming a Lost World.* Midlothian, Tex.: WIGTake Resources, 2004.

Greenleaf, Robert K. *Servant Leadership: A Journey into the Nature of Legitimate Power and Greatness.* New York: Paulist Press, 1977.

Guyot, Arnold. *Physical Geography.* Princeton, N.J.: Princeton Press, 1873.

Hall, Verna M. *The Christian History of the Constitution of the United States of America.* San Francisco: Foundation for American Christian Education, 1966.

Hinson, E. Glenn. *The Evangelization of the Roman Empire: Identity and Adaptability.* Macon, Ga.: Mercer University Press, 1981.

Howard, David M., ed. *Jesus Christ: Lord of the Universe, Hope of the World.* Downers Grove, Ill.: InterVarsity Press, 1974.

Jenkins, Philip. *The New Faces of Christianity: Believing the Bible in the Global South.* New York: Oxford University Press, 2006.

Jenkinson, William, and Helene O. Sullivan, eds. *Trends in Mission: Toward the Third Millennium.* Maryknoll, N.Y.: Orbis Books, 1993.

Johnson, Todd, and Kenneth R. Ross, eds. *The Atlas of Global Christianity 1910–2010.* Edinburgh: Edinburgh University Press, 2009.

Johnstone, Patrick. *The Church Is Bigger Than You Think.* Pasadena: William Carey Library, 1998.

————. *Operation World.* Bromley, UK: Send the Light Publishers, 2007.

Kane, J. Herbert. *Christian Missions in Biblical Perspective.* Grand Rapids: Baker Book House, 1976.

Kim, Djun Kil. *The History of Korea.* Westport, Conn.: Greenwood Press, 2005.

Kuyper, Abraham. *Lectures on Calvinism.* Grand Rapids: Eerdmans, 1931.

Latourette, Kenneth Scott. *A History of Christianity, Volume 1: To A.D. 1500.* New York: Harper & Row, 1975.

————. *A History of Christianity, Volume 2: A.D. 1500–A.D. 1975.* New York: Harper & Row, 1975.

Lawrence, Carl, and David Wang. *The Coming Influence of China.* Gresham, Ore.: Vision House, 1996.

Lloyd-Sidle, Patricia, and Bonnie Sue Lewis, eds. *Teaching Mission in a Global Context.* Louisville, Ky.: Geneva Press, 2001.

Lyall, Leslie T. *A World to Win.* London: InterVarsity Press, 1972.

McGavran, Donald A. *The Bridges of God: A Study in the Strategy of Missions.* New York: Friendship Press, 1955.

————. *How Churches Grow: The New Frontiers of Mission.* New York: Friendship Press, 1959.

Mangalwadi, Vishal. *Truth and Transformation: A Manifesto for Ailing Nations.* Seattle: YWAM Publishing, 2009.

Medlycott, A. E. *India and the Apostle Thomas.* London: Cambridge Publishers, 1905.

Menzies, Gavin. *1421: The Year China Discovered America.* New York: Perennial, 2004.

Micklethwait, John, and Adrian Wooldridge. *God Is Back: How the Global Revival of Faith Is Changing the World.* New York: Penguin Press, 2009.

Miller, Darrow L. *Discipling Nations: The Power of Truth to Transform Cultures.* Seattle: YWAM Publishing, 2001.

————. *LifeWork: A Biblical Theology for What You Do Every Day.* Seattle: YWAM Publishing, 2009.

Mott, John R. *Cooperation and the World Mission.* London: Student Christian Movement Press, 1935.

Neill, Stephen. *A History of Christianity in India: The Beginnings to AD 1707.* New York: Cambridge University Press, 1984.

Orr, J. Edwin. *The Eager Feet: Evangelical Awakenings, 1790–1830.* Chicago: Moody Press, 1975.

————. *Evangelical Awakenings in Africa.* Minneapolis: Bethany Fellowship, 1975.

————. *Evangelical Awakenings in Southern Asia.* Minneapolis: Bethany Fellowship, 1975.

————. *Evangelical Awakenings in the South Seas.* Minneapolis: Bethany Fellowship, 1976.

————. *Evangelical Awakenings in Latin America.* Minneapolis: Bethany Fellowship, 1978.

————. *The Re-Study of Revival and Revivalism.* Oxford: Oxford Press, 1981.

Pocock, Michael, Gailyn Van Rheenen, and Douglas McConnell. *The Changing Face of Missions: Engaging Contemporary Issues and Trends.* Grand Rapids: Baker Academic, 2005.

Pollock, J. C. *Hudson Taylor and Maria: Pioneers in China.* Grand Rapids: Zondervan, 1976.

Robeck, Cecil M., Jr. *The Azusa Street Mission and Revival: The Birth of the Global Pentecostal Movement.* Nashville: Thomas Nelson, 2006.

Schlafer, Dale. *An Urgent Appeal.* Westminster, Colo.: National Revival Network, 2001.

Shelley, Bruce L. *Church History in Plain Language.* Waco, Tex.: Word, 1982.

Sproul, R. C., and Archie Parrish. *The Spirit of Revival: Discovering the Wisdom of Jonathan Edwards.* Wheaton, Ill.: Crossway Books, 2000.

Stark, Rodney. *Discovering God: The Origins of the Great Religions and the Evolution of Belief.* New York: HarperOne, 2007.

———. *For the Glory of God: How Monotheism Led to Reformations, Science, Witch-Hunts, and the End of Slavery.* Princeton, N.J.: Princeton University Press, 2003.

Stier, Jim, Richlyn Poor, and Lisa Orvis, eds. *His Kingdom Come: An Integrated Approach to Discipling the Nations and Fulfilling the Great Commission.* Seattle: YWAM Publishing, 2008.

Synan, Vinson. *The Holiness-Pentecostal Tradition: Charismatic Movements in the Twentieth Century.* Grand Rapids: Eerdmans, 1997.

Tari, Mel. *Like A Mighty Wind.* Houston: New Leaf Publishing, 2001.

Tucker, Ruth A. *From Jerusalem to Irian Jaya: A Biographical History of Christian Missions.* Grand Rapids: Zondervan, 1983.

Tuttle, Robert G. *John Wesley: His Life and Theology.* Grand Rapids: Zondervan, 1978.

Wacker, Grant. *The Functions of Faith in Primitive Pentecostalism.* New York: Cambridge University Press, 1984.

Winter, Ralph D., and Steven C. Hawthorne, eds. *Perspectives on the World Christian Movement: A Reader.* 4th ed. Pasadena: William Carey Library, 2009.

Wesley, John. *The Journal of John Wesley.* Chicago: Moody Press, 1972.

Woolsey, Andrew. *Duncan Campbell: A Biography.* London: Hodder and Stoughton, 1974.

Worcester, J. H., Jr. *David Livingstone: First to Cross Africa with the Gospel.* Chicago: Moody Press, 1988.

Yohannan, K. P. *Revolution in World Missions.* Carrollton, Tex.: Gospel for Asia Books, 2000.

Yousef, Mosab Hassan. *Son of Hamas: A Gripping Account of Terror, Betrayal, Political Intrigue, and Unthinkable Choice.* Carol Stream, Ill.: SaltRiver, 2010.

Yun, Brother. *The Heavenly Man.* Grand Rapids: Kregel Publications, 2002.

Questions for Reflection or Discussion

Chapter 1

1. What sea changes have you witnessed during your lifetime? Technological? Related to the church or missions work?

2. What kinds of spiritual changes are occurring in the world in the twenty-first century? Why do you think this is the case?

3. Which of the five "Exhibits" surprised you the most? Why? Which one most encouraged you that God is doing some amazing things?

4. In which part of the world are you most excited about the coming sea change in missions? How can you contribute to those changes?

Chapter 2

1. How does your view of history determine how you live? Judging by your life's path and priorities, what is your view of history?

2. Do you think the metaphor of "waves" is a good way to describe God's redemptive role in history? Why or why not?

3. Which Old Testament wave of salvation did you find most interesting or had you never thought about before?

4. The godly King Josiah ushered in a wave of national reformation during his reign. How can you apply the eight principles of his life to your involvement in your city, state, or nation?

Chapter 3

1. What are Jesus' four clear commands for the New Testament missionary enterprise? Which commands have you obeyed? To which have you given the least attention?

2. What were the three missional keys to success during the time of the early church? Which one do you need to focus on more in your life and ministry?

3.   What is the meaning of the word *providence*? What are some of God's providential acts in history? What instances of God's providence do you see in your own life story?

4.   What technological advances aided gospel outreach during the early church era? How do you see God using technology to advance missions work in the twenty-first century? (Some of the answers may be found in chapter 13.)

Chapter 4

1.   How are rising tides a metaphor for some of the factors behind world evangelization? Are rising tides always apparent, or can their effects sometimes be unseen?

2.   What is your definition of revival? Have you ever been in a time of revival or spiritual awakening? How did it affect you?

3.   Why is prayer an important part of missions? How can you deepen your prayer life to help advance Christian missions?

4.   Why is unity important in multiplying God's work around the world? Read and reflect on John 17.

5.   What insight did Arnold Guyot share that helps us understand history? Is God's providential guiding of history fixed? What is the place of human free will?

Chapter 5

1.   Why do you think God used Count Zinzendorf and the Moravians to prepare the world for the first wave of modern missions? What qualities or practices can we learn from the Moravians that will increase our missional success?

2.   Why is William Carey called the "father of modern missions"? Why was his book on world evangelism (*An Enquiry Into the Obligation of Christians to Use Means for the Conversion of the Heathens*) so important in changing the missions debate and focus? Why did Carey focus on the coastlands of India and the world?

3.   How did the Moravian Revival and the First Great Awakening help fuel the first wave of modern missions? What role did prayer play in these two revivals?

4.   What group of people made up the first wave of modern missions? Why was this the case? Why did *Time* magazine name Johann Gutenberg the greatest man of the past five hundred years? How did his invention change the world?

Chapter 6

1.   Was David Livingstone primarily a Christian missionary or just an adventurous explorer? Why did God lead him to evangelize and explore the *interior* of Africa?

2. What made J. Hudson Taylor one of the greatest mission strategists of all time? What techniques did he use that changed the approach of later missionary work?

3. Why do you think God used young people—the Student Volunteer Movement—as a major missions force during the second wave of modern missions? How is he still using young people today?

4. What are the links between the great revivals of the nineteenth century and the explosion of the second wave of modern missions? What is the importance of the Mt. Hermon and Edinburgh Conferences?

5. What was the most significant personnel addition of the Second Wave? What was the primary reason for it? Why does Latourette call the period of 1815–1914 "the Great Century" of Christian missions?

6. How did the Industrial Revolution aid the cause of missions? How might the Information Age accomplish similar things in the twenty-first century?

Chapter 7

1. Who were the three key mission innovators of the third wave of modern missions? What significant contribution did each person make?

2. What specialization occurred during the Third Wave? Which aspect of specialization impacted your own life?

3. Christianity went south and west during the third wave of modern missions. Why did this happen? Will it continue in the twenty-first century? Why or why not?

4. Why do you think Pentecostal missions exploded during the third wave of modern missions? Has the emphasis on the power of the Holy Spirit impacted you?

5. Are you or your church involved in reaching unreached peoples? What can you do to join this central thrust of the Third and Fourth Waves?

Chapter 8

1. Restate and summarize the first three waves in modern missions. Why were they necessary to pave the way for the fourth?

2. What is unique about the revivals of the twentieth century? What nation in the last seventy years has seen the greatest awakening of people to Christ? What does this mean for the twenty-first century?

3. Have any of the prayer movements or thrusts of the past forty years impacted you? How has a spirit of unity fueled and multiplied the streams of intercession worldwide?

4.   What new faces in missions emerged during the end of the Third Wave? Why is this significant? How have you been affected by this enlarging of the global missions force?

5.   What technological advances have greatly accelerated world evangelism in the past hundred years? Which one or ones are most important to you?

Chapter 9

1.   Discuss the missions movements shown in table 1. Which one or ones impacted your heritage (nationality), leading to your salvation in Christ?

2.   What change in Christian demographics has taken place in the past 250 years? Would William Carey recognize the world of today? Why or why not?

3.   Are we making progress in reaching the unreached people of the world? What can you and your church do to contribute to that end?

4.   What group of people is being added to the world's mission force? What will missionaries of the twenty-first century look like? From which countries will they most likely be sent?

Chapter 10

1.   What were the limitations of the first three waves of modern missions in terms of missionary personnel? How will this change in the fourth wave of modern missions?

2.   How can children and youth be involved in missional activities in the twenty-first century? How can you as a young person—or, as an adult, encourage youth to—join the fourth wave of modern missions?

3.   How can senior saints contribute during this era? Share some examples of younger and older people who have contributed recently to global missions.

Chapter 11

1.   The early church missionaries were primarily from what nationality or region of the world? The First Wave missionaries came mainly from what continent?

2.   How did missions personnel broaden during the Third Wave? What will be unique about the missionaries of the Fourth Wave?

3.   What two nations might be strategic in missions advance in the twenty-first century? What needs to happen for them to have global impact?

4.   Why are church planting movements important? How can you and your church participate in this vital method of multiplication during the fourth wave of modern missions?

Chapter 12

1. How many people identify themselves as Christians today? How many others have heard about Christ? How many have not?

2. Do you believe that twenty-first-century Christians can complete the Great Commission? Why or why not?

3. Why are projects like Call2All and Project 4K important? Is there an Omega Zone, a city, or a nation that God has laid on your heart?

4. Seek God about targeting a specific people or nation. Begin discovering their needs, praying for them, and reaching them for Jesus.

Chapter 13

1. How have the inventions of the radio and television increased our ability to reach the world for Christ? Has God used them in your life to disciple you or bring you to faith?

2. What is the most watched film of all time? Why is film such a powerful medium of storytelling?

3. What percentage of the world either can't read or prefers not to? How can orality methods fill that void?

4. How can the Digital Age transform missions outreach? How have the use of computers, the availability of the Internet, and the proliferation of cell phones enhanced our ability to spread the gospel? How can you use these mediums in your own missional lifestyle?

Chapter 14

1. What is one of the major factors in the growth of relational evangelism today? Was a relational approach important in your conversion and/or discipleship?

2. How has the advent of television encouraged relational methods of communication? Will social networks be a force in the coming wave of missions? Why or why not?

3. Reflect on or share stories about how a high-touch, relational approach has impacted you or people you know. Who do you know that could use a gentle, compassionate revelation of Jesus? How can you reach out to them?

Chapter 15

1. Is there such a thing as an incomplete gospel? How have we hurt the advance of the gospel in past eras by preaching an incomplete message?

2. What does it mean to disciple a nation? When Jesus said he had all authority in heaven and on earth, how does that apply to various areas of human culture?

3.   Review the seven spheres of society. Why are these cultural leadership areas important? What happens to nations that aren't discipled fully in the ways of Christ?

4.   Do you feel called to one of the seven spheres? What steps can you take to bring the full teachings of Jesus Christ into this vital realm of society?

Chapter 16

1.   What five things can you do during the fourth wave of modern missions to live and act as a "World Christian"? Where is a good place to begin?

2.   What is your personal mission target or territory? What can you do to begin impacting a portion of the world for Christ?

3.   Which of the "missional stories" inspired you and why? How can you begin to live out your own story?

4.   In what ways can everyone be missional in the fourth wave of modern missions?

Chapter 17

1.   How can you cultivate a missional attitude in yourself and others?

2.   How must we reform Christian education to involve students in the Fourth Wave? What can you do at your church, fellowship, or school to contribute to that end?

3.   What are the remaining tasks of global evangelization? Visit the websites listed in the appendix and begin to learn more about how you can get involved.

4.   After you pray and do your research, adopt an unreached people and make them a focus during your lifetime. Pray for them. Give financially to those working among them. Take vacations in your nation of choice. Remember that you are the generation that may witness the return of our King.